The Little Book of Gold
Fundraising for Small and Very Small Nonprofits
By Erik Hanberg

*"It was a perfect primer for me as I prepare
for a new role in my agency."*
— **Anne Maack, Child Start**, Wichita, KS

*"A valuable contribution to our colleagues
in the nonprofit world—especially those of us in smaller
organizations that do not have dedicated fund development staff."*
— **Jose Martinez, Executive Director, Food Bank of
Yolo County**, Yolo County, CA

The Little Book of Gold
Fundraising for Small and Very Small Nonprofits
By Erik Hanberg
Copyright © 2009 by Erik Hanberg

ISBN-13: 978-1475205213
ISBN-10: 147520521X

TABLE OF CONTENTS

PREFACE

—⟨m⟩—

Why This Book Is "Little"

Answer #1 — This book is "little" for a lot of reasons. But the most basic answer is: this book is "little" because your nonprofit is little. This book is tailored to small and very small nonprofits who need effective fundraising solutions on a shoestring budget with a minimum amount of time invested.

Everything in here is in pursuit of that goal.

So, this book is "little" because you won't find long chapters covering ideas that you can't put into practice easily and efficiently. What works for a multimillion dollar hospital, a 100-year-old museum, or a prestigious college isn't necessarily going to work for you. We'll just stick to what we know works for small organizations and not waste time with the stuff that won't apply to you.

Since you may be wondering how big a "small" or "very small" nonprofit actually is, I'll give you my working definitions.

Small and very small nonprofits have an annual budget is a few hundred thousand dollars a year—maybe as much as a million. Whatever the budget, small nonprofits usually don't have a full-time employee dedicated to fundraising.

If you're a very small nonprofit, you bring in less than $100,000 a year, probably more like $25,000, and maybe even as little as $5,000. If you're making less than that, you need to consider whether you want to grow into something bigger or whether you are perfectly content to remain a loosely affiliated band of volunteers with a dedicated but narrow mission. And think carefully! Sometimes extremely small nonprofits can perform a valuable and targeted service to the community with grace and style in a way larger organizations can't.

Answer #2 — This book is "little" because what you need is a map, not an encyclopedia.

Large encyclopedic references of fundraising ideas have their place, but I'm guessing that's not what you need. Not only do you not have the time to read it, but what you need more than a list is a process. A place to start, followed by good, practical steps.

Individual ideas can be great, but unless they're plugged into a good system, they can work only so well. This book is about building that internal system from the ground up—a map for the future of fundraising at your nonprofit. It's a system designed for small and very small nonprofits, but it can also be a foundation for something much bigger if your organization has lofty dreams.

ANSWER #3 — This book is "little" because you should keep it with you.
My favorite book about writing is *The Elements of Style* by William Strunk and E.B. White. Packed with a few short rules, some clear guidelines, and a short essay on style, it makes its case succinctly and then lets you get on with the actual task of writing. Best of all, it's small enough it can fit into a coat pocket. I carry it with me because it has helped me more with writing than any other single book.

Now, if *The Little Book of Gold* could do for fundraising what *The Elements of Style* did for writing, I would die a happy man. More realistically, though, I hope you will carry this book with you because it describes an evolving and cyclical process, and you'll want to refer to it as you move forward.

Pull it out in those random moments when your brain needs a break between meetings or phone calls. Check to see what comes next on the road map. Find that section you've been thinking about. Or just flip through it randomly, looking for a sentence to strike you in a way it didn't the first time.

LITTLE BOOK, BIG IDEAS
Within these few pages, we'll tackle some of the trickiest pieces of fundraising: board giving, donor databases, donor cultivation, and event planning. We'll do it using effective and simple ideas that have already been tested by small nonprofits.

With any luck, you'll finish this book feeling as if you're ready to tackle the world and raise millions of dollars for your organization. Great! Keep that feeling.

But—while millions of dollars would be great—let's channel that energy toward a goal a little more realistic: let's raise $1,000.

PART ONE

A Year of Development

CHAPTER 1

Planning Ahead

FUNDRAISING IS NOT as scary as it sounds. But it's foreign to many people in small and very small nonprofits.

We follow our passions into community theater, our local environment, literacy, women's health, or our faith, and we find ourselves at a small nonprofit, doing a great amount of good. But we likely aren't there because we've followed our passion for ... fundraising.

Fundraising, when done right, is there to help you with what you really love: the mission of your nonprofit. Because I know you'd rather be doing something else, this book will focus on low-labor and low-cost fundraising strategies.

You can do this! Don't just throw up your hands in despair and hire someone. The temptation of all nonprofit managers is to delegate that which they like least, or feel least confident about, to someone else. As a result, some nonprofits will hire a development director long before it makes sense and never see the true potential of fundraising because too much of what they earn goes to staff they don't need (yet).

Small nonprofit directors should be actively involved in all aspects of an organization, especially when it's something like fundraising which accounts, for so much of your annual budget.

My Story

The first time I was asked to do any fundraising, I was 22 years old and barely two weeks into my new job. The target: $10,000 from a large corporation in Tacoma to be an event sponsor.

It was trial by fire. I spent hours preparing facts and figures. I made a chart on foam core, trying to understand what the directors of this multinational corporation would like to hear from me.

Finally, the day of the presentation arrived. I walked, foam core presentation in hand, to their towering office building. I shook hands with a small room full of senior executives and set up my presentation board.

Two minutes into my speech, a senior vice president interrupted me. "I'm sorry to interrupt," he said. "But we think this a fabulous event and we already know we want to sponsor at the $10,000 level. We don't need a pitch."

Waves of relief washed over me. It was the easiest gift I would ever solicit, but it was also the one I worried about the most.

Later in my nonprofit career I was hired to run the Grand Cinema, a nonprofit art-house cinema in downtown Tacoma. I couldn't help but remember that first big gift ask. Fundraising was to be an integral part of my job, and the part I was looking forward to the least.

With the help of some great mentors, long seminars, and simple trial and error, I was able to increase giving from about $17,000 per year to more than $80,000 in about two and a half years. Best of all, I did it with a minimum of effort, working my fundraising around the main business of presenting movies and our other film programming.

I'll get to the core principles that success was based on in a moment. But know that these are repeatable and strong foundations for low-cost, low-labor fundraising efforts.

I've taken that experience and applied it at other nonprofits as an executive director, a volunteer, and as a board member. I've worked in development at a multimillion-dollar nonprofit during a capital campaign. And I now sit on the distribution committee of a local foundation, giving away money to some of the very nonprofits I used to work for.

The experience of interviewing nonprofits during grant requests has strengthened my belief that these fundraising techniques can be effective for a variety of small nonprofits, no matter the mission. (My personal bias is toward arts nonprofits, but I'll use other examples as well throughout the book.)

Some nonprofits really have all their fundraising ducks in a row, and others seem to have little idea where they're going—all they know is that they need $2,000 by the end of the year ... or whatever amount their bookkeeper says they're short.

Don't be one of those nonprofits!

FIRST STEPS: THE PLAN

What you need is a plan for the year. It doesn't have to be anything fancy. In fact, the goal of this book is to provide you all the steps you'll need. By the end of it, you should have a clear sense of what the next year of fundraising will look like for you and your nonprofit.

The strategy we use will sound simple, but the truth is many nonprofits ignore it, or don't even know of it. If you are already raising money, you'll want to harness that effort toward the best use possible. And if you're new to fundraising, I want to start you off on the right foot. Here are some of the guiding principles at the core of successful, professional fundraising.

START CLOSE AND WORK OUTWARD

The most effective fundraising is done with people who already know what your nonprofit is about. It is very difficult to tell someone about what you do while asking for money at the same time. By starting with the closest people to your nonprofit, you are starting with the most likely givers and moving slowly out from there. This is, in fact, the structure of Part I of this book and how we recommend spending your first year of professional development: start with the board, then "friends" of the nonprofit, and then use a fundraising event to increase contacts from the general public and bring them into your circle.

WORK SMARTER, NOT HARDER

As a small nonprofit, you probably don't have any staff dedicated to fundraising. That means you're trying to squeeze it in around the other important work you do. The solution is not to delegate fundraising, as many nonprofit managers are tempted to do, but rather to make it as effective as absolutely possible. We'll be looking at highly effective fundraising techniques. Don't be tempted by chocolate bar sales, bake sales, or other high-labor/low return fundraising.

To know for sure that you're working "smarter," you should keep track of all your hours spent on fundraising. We'll compare that regularly to what you bring in as your "hourly rate."

Some nonprofit managers might find that they are spending so many hours on such bad fundraisers that their hourly rate is *negative*—that is, a manager paid $20/hour is raising money at a rate of $10/hour. You can do better. In fact, you can do a lot better.

ALL YOU'VE GOT IS YOUR REPUTATION

When famed investor Warren Buffett took over a failing investment company recovering from a major scandal, he told his new employees, "Lose money for the firm, and I will be understanding. Lose a shred of reputation for the firm, and I will be ruthless."

Buffett's focus on reputation applies just as much to small nonprofits as it does large institutions, if not more so. Why? Because your reputation is all you've got. A large hospital, a large university, a large corporation, has assets and resources to keep it afloat while it rebuilds a sullied reputation. It can rebrand, it can launch a PR blitz, it can work through it.

Your organization may not have that luxury.

Donors should expect the most from the nonprofits that they give to. If you violate trust with a donor, you have put your organization at risk. You should be aware of the Donor Bill of Rights, which was developed by the Giving Institute, Association for Healthcare Philanthropy, Council for Advancement and Support of Education, and the Association of Fundraising Professionals. I have reprinted it below.

DONOR BILL OF RIGHTS

Philanthropy is based on voluntary action for the common good. It is a tradition of giving and sharing that is primary to the quality of life. To assure that philanthropy merits the respect and trust of the general public, and that donors and prospective donors can have full confidence in the not-for-profit organizations and causes they are asked to support, we declare that all donors have these rights:

1. *To be informed of the organization's mission, of the way the organization intends to use donated resources, and of its capacity to use donations effectively for their intended purposes.*

2. *To be informed of the identity of those serving on the organization's governing board, and to expect the board to exercise prudent judgment in its stewardship responsibilities.*

3. *To have access to the organization's most recent financial statements.*

4. *To be assured their gifts will be used for the purposes for which they were given.*

5. *To receive appropriate acknowledgment and recognition.*

6. *To be assured that information about their donations is handled with respect and with confidentiality to the extent provided by law.*

7. *To expect that all relationships with individuals representing organizations of interest to the donor will be professional in nature.*

8. *To be informed whether those seeking donations are volunteers, employees of the organization or hired solicitors.*

9. *To have the opportunity for their names to be deleted from mailing lists that an organization may intend to share.*

10. *To feel free to ask questions when making a donation and to receive prompt, truthful and forthright answers.*

In short: be scrupulous.

Spend Later

If your nonprofit is new to the organized, professional fundraising that will be introduced in this book, you stand to earn a good deal more in donations than you have before.

With that in mind, the best budgeting practice you could adopt is to wait to spend that money until next year. (Sorry, but it's true.) Let's say that you normally raise $5,000 a year from donors. And after reading this book and implementing the concepts in it, you increase that to $15,000 for this fiscal year. *Save it for the next year.* That extra $10,000 was money you didn't expect. Now that you've raised it, you know exactly how much you can spend the next year—$15,000.

And then next year, while you're spending the $15,000 from this year, let's say you've increased giving again to $20,000. Spend that a year later.

The power of this structure is that if circumstances outside your control undercut fundraising (like a recession or a major disaster), you are not facing a deficit at the end of the year and won't find yourself needing to raise $10,000 in a month. Instead, you will have a year to make the necessary cuts in reaction to lower giving.

If your nonprofit is disciplined enough to follow this model, you won't find yourself in do-or-die fundraising scenarios that so often plague small nonprofits.

The hardest part is making the switch, and the best time to do it is when giving increases. Put off spending it, and your nonprofit becomes that much more secure.

CHAPTER 2

—⁓—

BOARD GIVING: YOUR FIRST $1,000

A S I SAID in the last chapter, we're going to start our fundraising with the people closest to the nonprofit and work outward from there.

This chapter deals with board and staff giving, Chapter 3 with friends and contacts of the nonprofit, Chapter 4 with fundraising events that bring in new contacts, and Chapter 5 tackles "major gifts"—taking your largest donors and asking them to increase it.

Put together, these chapters will serve as a *development plan* for the year, and a foundation for all future years.

STARTING WITH THE BOARD OF DIRECTORS

Does your board give generously and regularly?

Most likely not. In theory, giving should start with the board of directors. But in practice, this is seldom the case—especially at small nonprofits.

Why is this?

Small nonprofit boards frequently like to call themselves "working boards" to differentiate themselves from "fundraising boards." When someone tells you, "We're not a fundraising board," what they're telling you is that the board is not composed of "big name" community members who cut checks left and right. Using this definition, a working board is one in which the volunteers are passionate about their cause; aren't afraid to roll up their sleeves and do some actual work, and donate time and talent, but don't part with much treasure.

In my experience, boards that think of themselves as a "working board" think they've done enough just by sitting on a board and helping the organization.

This couldn't be further from the truth.

First, the board of directors should be the most committed to an organization's success. Sometimes it doesn't feel that way, because the board is privy to all the behind-the-scenes squabbles and dilemmas the general public doesn't see. But a board member should be one of the most likely donors to an organization.

If this doesn't feel true at your nonprofit, you're in need of a cultural change. Cultural changes can sometimes take ages. But they can also be swift if tackled in the right way.

Let's go through the steps that will make your "working board" a significant part of fundraising as well.

Meet Linda

To illustrate this process (and later ideas as well), I'm going to turn to "Linda." Linda has spent a year as the executive director of a nonprofit dedicated to preserving the history of Smallville, USA. The organization she runs, the Smallville Historical Society, operates a historic cabin that has been preserved since the days of the pioneers. Linda supervises two employees and a handful of volunteers who give tours of a pioneer cabin. All in all, the organization has an annual budget of $100,000.

But times have gotten tight at the Historical Society. There are fewer volunteers than there used to be; fewer patrons seem to be paying the suggested donation of $5 per person on weekends; and Linda is worried she will have to lay off her part-time bookkeeper. Linda believes the key to surviving a tight year and improving the Historical Society is more aggressive fundraising. Everyone seems to like the Historical Society— at least, those who have heard of it—so she wants to be careful that she doesn't make people feel "hit up" for money, either. So how to proceed?

The Board Comes First

Linda's goal is to get 100% of the board giving to the Historical Society. One grant she wants to apply for requires 100% giving. But she doesn't want to just tell the board that everyone needs to give and end up getting a handful of $20 donations.

She wants the board to be proud of their gifts as a whole. If the board feels good about their cumulative giving, she figures, their friends and other donors will be more likely to give.

The other reason Linda is starting with the board is that it's the easiest and cheapest way for her to reach potential donors. There are nine people on her board, all of whom are clearly familiar with the nonprofit. They already care about it, and some of them have given in the past. Even better, they meet monthly, so it's never too hard to reach them. And she can use the power of the group to get everyone committed to giving.

All that's left is to ask ...

Of course, "the ask" is the scariest part. Linda's never actually asked for a gift for the organization the entire time she's led the organization. Sure, she's applied for grants, and she spent a lot of time working on the annual auction. But she's never actually asked someone to give.

ASKING WITHOUT ASKING

Linda decides she needs to get the board in a better place. She's terrified of making the ask, and she has a pretty good idea that the board isn't very interested in shelling out a lot of money. What she needs to do is change both how she thinks about asking for money and how the board feels about giving it.

She has one major advantage over the board, though: information.

STEP 1: CALL YOUR BOARD CHAIR

Linda calls her board chair and tells him that she wants to spend some time at the next board meeting updating the board about the state of donations as the organization enters the last quarter of the year. (If it's in the last quarter of the year, use the end of the year as your excuse. If it's the last quarter of your fiscal year, use that. If it's the first quarter of your fiscal year, that could work, too. You get the idea.)

He agrees, and mentions that he's been wondering about fundraising himself. Can we make the auction bigger, he asks. Linda's already pretty sure she doesn't want to spend even more of her year planning the auction, but she tells him that she'll be making a thorough presentation.

She also tells him that she will be letting the board know she wants to see the board get to 100% giving. Of course, no one will be expected to give at the meeting. She just wants to alert them that this goal will be mentioned. (You can sometimes surprise a board member with new things, but as a rule of thumb, you should never surprise your board chair in front of the board.)

STEP 2: RESEARCH!

Now with a deadline, Linda starts preparing. She doesn't think the board will respond to a big elaborate presentation and slideshow. So she decides to give them a short update of facts and then lead a good discussion. But first she needs the facts.

Here are the questions she decides she wants to answer:

- *How much money has been raised in the last year?*

- *How many donors did that come from?*

- *What was the largest gift? The average gift? The most common gift? (slightly different than the average gift, but often just as helpful)*

- *How many board members gave?*

Many organizations have a database of donors and can get these questions with a snap of their fingers. Linda doesn't, so she creates one in Excel.

If you don't have a database, don't be scared about creating one on your own. By purchasing this book, you now have access to online downloads, including a template for a *donor database* and a guidebook for using it. All downloads are online at **www.thelittlebookofgold. com/index.php/downloads**.

Linda has her bookkeeper pull records from the auction, from stray donation checks that have arrived, and from the cash and checks collected at the door of the Pioneer Cabin.

From this point on, it's just a data entry job. Instead of assigning her bookkeeper to it, though, Linda decides it's worth the time to spend a couple of hours entering the numbers herself. It gives her some time to look at the names on the list. Some names jump out at her. One board member who always complains about things is actually one of the biggest donors. And there are two checks from a family Linda knows to be very wealthy: one donation came during a tour and a check for a larger donation came three weeks later.

With her data entered, Linda is now in a place to start answering her questions.

HOW MUCH MONEY HAS BEEN RAISED IN THE LAST YEAR?

In the last year, the Historical Society received about $9,000 in donations from individuals through all its fundraising activities. But $2,000 of that came in the form of cash at the door of the Pioneer Cabin, and Linda can't identify who gave it. And $500 came from a raffle at the auction and she doesn't have records on who bought tickets. In addition to money from the individual donors, the society received $15,000 in grants.

It's important to know total giving for your organization, but it's also important to know the breakdown between grants and individual giving. A grant from a foundation for tens of thousands of dollars is very different from an individual's gift of the same amount.

Also important is to compare total giving with the total revenue of your nonprofit. Does your organization have any earned income—fees, subscriptions, retail sales, tickets, etc.—separate from donations? One often-quoted rule of thumb is that donations should make up no more than 60% of revenue. It's less a hard and fast rule and more a suggestion: be careful if your organization is overly reliant on any single source of funding. If too much comes from one area, whether grants, donations, or ticket sales, it's a good idea to put some work into boosting performance in other areas.

For the Historical Society, out of the $100,000 budget, $24,000 was donated. The rest of the income was split between contracts with the state and the parks department to maintain the grounds of the cabin, revenue generated from school tours, and limited retail at the cabin.

HOW MANY DONORS DID THAT COME FROM?

Since Linda couldn't say for sure where $2,500 of her $9,000 in giving came from, she just tallied the remaining $6,500, which came from 250 donors.

WHAT WAS THE LARGEST GIFT? THE AVERAGE GIFT? THE MOST COMMON GIFT?

Linda discovered that she had two gifts of $250, 3 of $100, 20 of $50, and all the remaining were right around $20, resulting from their $5/person suggested donation. Linda had seen a lot of families of four come through, so she wasn't surprised to see so many checks for $20. It was also the ticket price on the auction, though Linda wasn't sure it could all count as a donation since the auction certainly didn't make $20 per person (and she would be right, but her organization's books weren't set up to account for the difference).

So her largest gift was $250. The average gift was $26. And the most common gift was $20. Linda felt for the first time that she actually had a handle on how fundraising looked at her organization. It was a relief to have it sorted out.

At the same time, it was rather surprising. Volunteers kept a tally of attendees at the cabin. She'd never done the math before, but between the checks and the cash collected at the door, she had collected only $6,000 at the door from the 4,000 tallied. That was only a $1.50/person instead of the hoped-for $5!

Linda's experience is pretty typical. She was a good steward of the nonprofit's resources, but she never had really done any analysis. Now, with only about four hours of work, she felt that she had a better grasp of the organization's fundraising than she'd had in the year since she started. *And* she'd discovered a significant problem: the cabin wasn't collecting nearly as much money as it should be. She felt bad about that one. After all, she knew attendance totals off the top of her head. And she knew how much money the cabin pulled in—she had to report it to the board monthly. But she had never actually *compared* the numbers.

She felt a little better when she realized that no one on the board had compared the numbers either. Everyone had just *assumed* that the Pioneer Cabin was going to be a small part of the budget. But Linda realized that if she could actually get $5 from every person who came, they would make $20,000 from the cabin, an increase of $14,000. What they could do with that money! With just a little bit of data entry and critical thinking, Linda had discovered information that totally changed how she thought about one part of her organization. Too many people shy away from what they consider menial work. Spend a little time doing it and you may find assumptions challenged and new questions to ask.

The other important part of Linda's experience was discovering that donors to the Historical Society formed a sort of pyramid. She had a handful of generous donors, a larger group of mid-range donors, and a wide base of small gifts. The actual numbers that fill out the pyramid will be different depending on the size of your nonprofit and the maturity of previous fundraising. But it will probably look like a pyramid.

Of course there are always exceptions. I worked with a large nonprofit that made targeted annual asks of $4,000. It was a specific amount for a specific reason, but we ended up with a bubble in the middle of our pyramid. Your organization may have a similar bubble or a similar contraction.

We'll talk more about donor pyramids in Chapter 5 and why they can be so helpful.

HOW MANY BOARD MEMBERS GAVE?

Linda flagged each board member when she entered her donation. Now she looked at all their information together. Of the nine, only five had given. One had given $250, and the other four had given $50 each. Although almost all of them came to the auction, none had paid because they were on the board.

Linda also recorded the dates of gifts when she entered them into her spreadsheet. Most of the board members had written checks a couple months after she'd started when the board chair had mentioned in passing that it would be good for the board to give. Some people had written checks at the meeting. The rest said they would mail a check in. Only one did. And, Linda realized with a bit of anger, the board chair wasn't one of the five!

STEP 3: THE PRESENTATION

Before doing her research, Linda felt nervous about approaching the board for money. Now she felt fired up and her biggest concern was controlling her excitement, not getting up the nerve.

She'd planned ahead well. Linda stood up in front of the board of directors. Normally she would have sat with them, but this seemed like an opportune time to be in front of them as a leader. She was a little concerned that one person had missed the meeting, but she started off anyway.

"I just wanted to give everyone an update on the state of our fundraising. It's already the end of September and with the end of the year and next year's budgeting coming up, I thought it was a good time to look at this information together.

"First, before we get into the specifics, I want to try a short exercise with everyone here." Linda passed out scraps of paper and pencils to everyone. "I want you to answer a question for me. What would you consider a 'large' gift to the Historical Society? If I were to come in next month and say to you, 'Great news! We just got a check in the mail and it's for *blank* amount,' how much would it have to be, for you to say, 'Wow, that's a large gift'?"

Everyone wrote down an amount and Linda collected them. She wrote their numbers up on a white board. They were: $1,000, $1,000, $500, $500, $500, $500, $100, and $20,000. When she got to the last one, Linda looked at the man known to be a bit of a rebel who seemed to enjoy being irritating.

"Was that yours, John?" she asked.

Everyone laughed and John said, "Well, $20,000 would be large. The rest are just chump change."

Linda laughed and said, "I think for the purposes of this I'll make one small edit." She erased the last zero off $20,000, dropping it to $2,000. "This will make averaging these a little easier, and yours is still the highest, John." Adding them up and dividing by eight, Linda wrote the average on the board: $762.50.

"Looking at this, on average you thought $762.50 was large. But since half of you thought $500 was a large gift, I think we should count that number, too. So it would take a gift of at least $500 to be a 'large' gift."

Linda paused, partly for dramatic effect and partly because she wanted to collect her thoughts.

"Well, I agree, $500 would be a large gift. In fact, it would be larger than any gift we received in the last year ... which is why I wanted to update everyone on where we stand today. In fact, the largest gift we received last year was $250, and we only got two of those. We need to identify people who could someday give us $500."

Linda had thought ahead and planned a couple of different contingencies. She didn't know what people would write down: would everyone write $100, or would everyone write $1,000? She planned on different responses depending on how things averaged out. She also knew that John would probably not cooperate well, so she decided that if that happened, she'd try to keep it light and humorous.

"Now, we may not have had many big gifts, but we did have a lot of small gifts, and that's good, too. Last year 235 people gave us $20 between the Pioneer Cabin and the auction. Having those small donors gives me a lot of hope that we can make some of them our big donors later. In addition to all that, we received $3,000 in cash, which means I can't identify who it came from.

"In total, that's $9,000 donated to us in the last year. Does anyone have any questions or should I move on to my plan for how to increase this over the next 12 months?"

Notice a couple of things: Linda didn't ask for ideas to increase giving. You probably already know that boards love to give ideas. But a board meeting is not the place to brainstorm fundraising ideas. That's how you end up with a bake sale or a stressful auction.

Notice, too, that she dangled her plan in front of them like a cliffhanger. Not only will this likely keep questions limited, but she also reinforced that she's in control of the situation, which again will help keep brainstorming at bay.

With only a few questions from the board—most Linda answered by saying "I'll get to that in a second"—Linda was ready to move on.

"I think we need to have two main goals. The first is to expand the number of small donations we get. We'll want to figure out ways to collect more names and addresses at the pioneer cabin. In fact, I think we need to look more closely at how we collect donations there, in general. At next month's meeting, I'd like to focus on that and provide some recommendations.

"I think it's time to attempt an *annual campaign* and to ask people to donate. We have a lot of names and addresses of people who have supported us in the past. We know they like us. I think that before the end of the year we should plan to send them a letter and ask for their support."

This would be a first for the Historical Society. Even if your organization has had a regular annual fund before, the next part of Linda's proposal is still probably new.

"And that's where I need the board's help. I really want to do this right, and I want our donors to feel appreciated. I'd like a board member to call every donor who gives more than $50 and thank them for their donation. At that level, everyone will probably call two or three donors and thank them. I think a phone call from a board member would really make a donor feel that they did something special, even if it's just a voicemail from you."

For the Historical Society, a call to donors at the $50 level makes sense, since there are so few at $50 and above. At your organization, the cutoff may be at $100 or $250. Figure that each board member shouldn't be responsible for calling more than 3 or 4 people, and work backwards from there.

For the board members, it's such a low time commitment they should have a hard time saying no. Also, they're not *asking* for money, they're thanking a donor, and that's a lot easier.

Linda's board seemed genuinely excited about the idea. Now was the right time to move on to the next phase: board giving.

STEP 4: ASKING WITHOUT ASKING (FINALLY!)

Linda took a breath and proceeded.

"Now, I think that if you're picking up the phone to thank someone for donating, you should probably be a donor yourself." Linda laughed a little bit to keep the mood light. "I'd like to be able to put in the letter that we have 100% board and staff participation. I don't want any checks from you tonight. I'd like to give everyone a chance to go home and talk it over with anyone they need to. We can handle the gift part later in the month."

Everyone seemed to think that handling it later was better.

Linda kept going. "I would really like people to think on a gift that would be significant for them. Obviously, I'm not saying that it should be like these numbers," Linda said, waving at the results of the exercise she'd done before. "Although if John wants to give $20,000, I think we'd take it." Everyone laughed.

"Speaking for myself, the only way I will be able to make a significant gift is to donate it in monthly installments. So I hope you will consider a *recurring gift* as an option, too.

"And when we meet again next month, I'd really like to be able to report back with 100% board *and staff* giving!"

Linda was scared during this last part, but she got through it. She had gotten everyone ready to be asked later. Broaching the subject now, but not actually doing the asking yet, meant that the next time Linda talks to each of them, there wouldn't be any surprise. She'd also gotten them thinking about "large" and "significant" gifts. She thought she was unlikely to get anything at $500, a couple might give at $250, but what she was really hoping for was at least $100 from everyone.

She'd also brought herself in as a donor. Just as she argued that the board members who thank donors should be donors as well, she realized that she would get a lot more leverage later if she were a donor, too. Sorry, but it's true. You should be ready to give at least $10/month back to the nonprofit. Try to get close to whatever you think a majority of board members will give.

ANOTHER OPTION: SET A GOAL

If the Historical Society had more established board giving, Linda could have taken this opportunity to set a goal for the board. (You usually need regular board giving to use this method, because you need the previous data to help you set the goal. Try to peg what nine board members will give as a whole—without any data—and you will likely overshoot or undershoot.)

Asking for a cumulative goal has a couple benefits: it sets a goal for the board that they get to feel good about reaching. It also doesn't assume that everyone is going to give equally to get there. One board member might give half of the total, even. If you have board members with very different means, this allows the entire board to feel good about the cumulative goal.

There are some pitfalls to setting goals, however. A large goal might scare board members, especially if it's coming from the executive director. To get around this, the board chair should probably be the one making the pitch at the meeting, and describing how the goal was put together.

Also, to make a large goal sound less scary, the board chair should already have *pledged* a gift, and the two of you should have already sat down and asked the largest donor on the board to pledge a gift as well (using the major gift skills discussed in Chapter 5). This means that when you say, "our goal is $2,000" you won't scare anyone because you follow it up with, "and we're already $700 of the way there."

And Now ... The Ask

Linda left the board meeting feeling good. A couple of board members said they were impressed at the information she'd collected. One board member gave her a check. She accepted it without looking at the amount, but said, "Would it be all right if we still met for coffee anyway? I'd like to practice a bit before I get to the rest of the board members." The board member agreed, though Linda figured he had probably given the check trying to get out of the pitch. With that out of the way, it was time to get to the actual ask.

Step 1: Make an Appointment with the Board Chair

Linda called her board chair the next morning. She treated him like a confidant.

"It's more than just for the donation letter or particular grants that makes me want to increase board giving," Linda told him. "There's such potential to raise giving, and the board is so dedicated, starting with them might give us a good idea how we're going to do with everyone else."

He agreed.

"So do you think the two of us can sit down later this week or early next week? I'd like you to be my first meeting so I can practice a bit before I get to the rest of the board members."

She got the meeting scheduled.

Linda liked the "practice" line. She knew she couldn't use on it anyone who wasn't a board member, but she thought it might make it easier for her, and for them, to get behind the meetings. For her, she got to think of it as a chance to practice. Board members got to feel that they were helping her and the organization. And at the end of it, she'd still get a donation.

It was a trick that she knew could only work on certain members. For some of them, like the rebel John, she felt it would be disastrous. But it made it easier with the rest.

The key, she felt, was to be honest ... honest with a positive spin. For Linda that meant being up front with needing practice. For someone who has regularly made asks, it might mean something else. But staying honest and upbeat—essentially treating board members like donors, and not as someone *obligated* to give—made the board feel a lot better about giving.

STEP 2: SET UP A MERCHANT ACCOUNT

Linda had learned the hard way how difficult it was to run an auction without accepting credit cards. She thought of her own spending habits and realized that she rarely wrote checks anymore and put most things on a credit or debit card.

Linda knew there were plenty of companies that could set up a merchant account, but she wanted to save time. She went to the Historical Society's bank and was able to get a merchant account set up quickly.

She also found an app on her smart phone that would allow her to immediate process credit cards. There were a lot to choose from, but she chose Square (squareup.com), which allowed her to run cards directly on her phone.

STEP 3: THE FIRST ASK

Linda sat down at a local coffee shop to meet with the board chair. He had suggested lunch but she didn't want a long (and expensive) meal, so she was able to get a coffee meeting scheduled in the middle of the morning. She would have been equally content to meet him at his office. Either way, she wanted him to know that she was making the effort to meet him and didn't ask him to come to her.

After small talk, Linda opened the conversation: "The more I thought about it after the meeting, the more I liked the idea of getting the board on recurring gifts. It would help us with a lot of issues. Our cash flow would be more stable; board members could stretch their gift out over the year so it doesn't hurt their wallets as much; and we won't have to chase after them for their gift like we might with a pledge."

INTERLUDE TO STEP 3: RECURRING GIFTS VS. PLEDGES

A pledge is a commitment from a donor to give you money in the future. Most large nonprofits deal in pledges, but this is one of those times where what works for a large nonprofit can be trouble for a small organization.

A donor who pledges $500 often has to be reminded of the pledge. Nonprofits usually do this with billing statements so that they aren't hounding a donor over the phone. Billing statements have a cost, and sometimes a donor won't follow through, meaning that the nonprofit doesn't get the donation (or a part of the donation).

Recurring gifts are essentially pledges, in that the donor commits to give a certain amount of money in the future. But they also give you a means to collect the donation—like a credit or a debit card number.

(Note that both pledges and recurring gifts allow donors to give more than they would be able to give if they had to write you a check on the spot.)

The big benefit of recurring gifts is they allow a nonprofit to run a credit card number once a month without hounding the donor. They also are easier to renew because they don't require donors to do anything but agree to continue them (or raise them).

That said, recurring gifts aren't perfect, either. A $120 gift run 12 times in a year will also generate 12 charges on your merchant account, a higher cost than running that gift once, or even four times, since merchant accounts often have a small flat fee for each transaction. Also, like pledges, they can be canceled by the donor or the donor may max out the card's limit or have to switch cards because to identity theft. Then you have to follow up and get the information again.

I still like recurring gifts for small nonprofits. I think that getting the card numbers makes them a surer thing than a pledge. Also, a nonprofit using an Excel spreadsheet—or anything other than a true donor database—will find it difficult to accurately track pledges.

BACK TO STEP 3: THE FIRST ASK

The board chair agreed with Linda about the recurring gifts.

Linda continued, "What I'm really hoping for with the board is to schedule short coffee meetings like this one in the next month and get everyone giving $10 to $20 each month. Do you think we can make that goal?"

Linda was still treating her board chair like a confidant, which is good because she'll need a lot of support from him later. She also floated a range of gifts she's looking for with her board chair to test the waters.

"I don't know if we can get it from everyone," he said. "But I think we can get close to that range for a lot of them. It's actually close to what I was thinking about as well." The board chair said that he'd like to give $20 each month.

Linda was appropriately ecstatic. She pulled out a donation form that included a space for a credit card number and expiration date. "I want you to know that I have a lockbox in the office that only I and the bookkeeper have access to. No one else will be touching these numbers."

The board chair told Linda he didn't know the Historical Society could take credit cards, as he reached for his wallet. "I just set it up," she told him proudly.

As he was filling out the form, Linda said, "I agree with you that we may not be able to get into the range we want with every board member. It would really help me out if tonight or tomorrow you could find some time to call everyone—especially Susan since she missed the meeting. Just a quick call to let them know you feel this is really important, maybe stress the recurring gift, and that I'll be coming around to see them in the next few weeks."

"I can do that," he said. "Should I mention numbers or anything?"

"If they ask, you can allude to what you gave, but you don't have to. I would like you to consider coming to two of the coffee meetings if you have the time."

"Which two?"

Linda named John, her rebel board member, and the board member who gave $250 last year. The board chair agreed.

And that was that! Linda walked away with a $240 gift to be paid over the next year.

By the time she met her next board member, also for coffee, she felt more confident. This time, she adopted the "royal we" saying, "We are hoping to get all the board members on a recurring gift of $20/month."

And then she added, "Do you think you would be able to consider a gift in that range?"

Linda memorized that line for the first two board member meetings because she was so nervous saying it. She's followed a basic process of asking:

1. She went into the meeting with a specific dollar amount in mind (on the high end of what she thought the board member could do).

2. She asked for it politely and with confidence.

3. And then she had the hardest part ahead of her: remaining silent.

After asking for a gift, you should be prepared for one of the most uncomfortable silences of your life (that feeling goes away after practice). *It is not your job to break the silence.* Let the donor do that, when he or she responds. Anything you say after making the ask will hurt the size of the gift you'll get.

A NOTE ON NAMING FIGURES

It's important to point out here that naming a figure can sometimes be called a "hard sell" because you're putting the donor on the spot. The person can either agree to the figure you've named, offer a lower figure, or say no to any giving.

Asking for a specific figure can be a scary thing to do, but consider everything that led up to this ask from the board member's perspective:

- A presentation at the board about the importance of giving and the indication that members would be asked for a gift

- A phone call from the board chair telling them about the importance of giving

- A phone call from the executive director to schedule the meeting

- A personal meeting at a place convenient for the board member

That's actually a lot of *touches* for a gift of this size. It makes saying "no" harder in a good way—namely, the donor feels important, needed, and motivated to give.

You can't afford to do this for every gift of $240 that you want to solicit. But for a board of directors unaccustomed to giving regularly, putting a lot of personal touches into these asks can bring about the cultural change you are looking for. (If it's not clear yet, this is a good time to mention that the exact figures of this chapter will vary depending on your nonprofit. A gift of $240 or $500 is large for the Historical Society, but may be small change for your nonprofit. The figures aren't as important as the process.)

It's also important to note here that no matter what the donor said after Linda made the ask, she acted as if it was the most generous gift she'd received. There was no haggling or guilt. Whatever the donor named was the number she was looking for, even if it was half or less of what she'd floated.

In the end, Linda met with all nine board members over the course of a month. The time she invested was three to four hours of data entry/analysis on giving; two hours of thinking and preparation for the presentation; and then about one hour for each ask (counting the time to schedule the meeting and actually meet) for a total of 15 hours of work. For that, she got three recurring gifts of $20/month, four recurring gifts of $10/month, one check written on the spot for $250 (the same donor who gave $250 the year before), and a gift of $50 from a board member who pleaded that he just couldn't do more. That's a grand total of $1,500.

From the staff, she personally committed a gift of $10/month and got two one-time gifts of $50 from her two employees, raising the total amount of her board/staff campaign to $1,720, which took another hour. (Approaching staff can be a little scary for a manager as well. I recommend having a similar discussion about the importance of 100% as happened at the board meeting, possibly with the Board Chair present and giving the staff a form to fill out and return later, instead of committing to their boss on the spot, which can be awkward.)

All told, Linda worked 15 to 16 hours and raised $1720. That's more than $100 per hour. In the previous year, individual donations totaled $9,000. With less than 20 hours of work, Linda was on track to increase donations by 19%.

And she'd asked only 12 people.

Step 4: The Reward at the Next Meeting

When Linda came to at the next board meeting, she arrived bearing a large cake and bottles of sparkling cider. On the cake, written in frosting, was "100%."

While everyone ate cake, Linda announced the cumulative total without revealing anyone's individual gift. She thanked everyone for their gifts again. (Before the meeting, Linda and her board chair had each signed simple thank you cards and mailed them to the board. Linda also wrote a special note to the board chair for all the work he'd done). She commended the board on its achievement of the goal. She invited the board chair to also thank everyone (she had planned this with him ahead of time). And she promised that they would be moving on to more donors before the end of the year.

With board giving out of the way, Linda was ready to move on and look to the larger community.

Special Cases: It's Not Always Smooth Sailing

The general format Linda used after she got into a rhythm was pretty basic:

- Make sure there is no doubt about the purpose of the meeting.
- Make every effort to go to the board member instead of having them come to you.
- Include the board chair and get him to call ahead when possible as another touch.
- Treat the board member like a highly prized donor, even if there are personal issues she had with the board member or issues that board member had with the nonprofit.
- Float a specific goal. Can be a goal "for the board."
- Be quiet!
- Acknowledge the generosity of each gift, no matter the amount.
- Bring in the board chair for the best donors and the most likely "problem" board members.
- Thank the board as a whole and individually.

But there are different kinds of board members who may need a little extra finessing. Here are some thoughts on how to handle them.

Dealing With the Rebel

You know the type who takes the opposite view of the group, just to be contrarian. They like stirring up trouble, they like throwing bombs into conversations, and they get kicks from torpedoing meetings. Does your board have one of these people?

If so, I'm sorry. There's a difference between healthy dissent and being difficult for the sake of attention.

So how to get this person to give? You'll need your board chair with you for this one.

Rebels are just as likely to explain why they would never give as they are to explain why they want to give at a level of $5,000—but why you, the executive director, have lost that gift. They like being unpredictable.

My experience with "rebels" is that they choose some point and stick to it come hell or high water. Whatever issue they choose isn't the point: they just want a moral ground to argue from. So don't get too involved in the minutiae of their issue.

If after asking for a gift, the rebel puts up resistance, the hard talk should come from the board chair. It is not the executive director's job to lecture board members on their responsibility—it's the board chair's. Letting the board chair know in advance that you are worried about the rebel board member and talking through different arguments that might crop up is a good idea.

Note: don't accept conditional gifts! As in, "I'll give once you change your stance on ..." or "I'll give if you just let me be your volunteer marketing director." Bad, bad, bad, bad. Board members should never hold their money hostage.

Here are some good arguments your board chair can use with a rebel board member:

"John, I like a lot of what you said and it's good food for thought. I understand the critiques you've made as well. The Historical Society isn't perfect by any means, I agree. But despite any flaws, it's worthy of getting support from all of its board members. We can work out the issues later, but we need everyone's support right now."

If the rebel still balks ...

"As members of the community, we only have three things to donate: time, talent, and treasure. You have generously given your time and talent—in the form of wisdom and insight—to the Historical Society. But being on the board of directors means giving all three. It's what being on the board of directors means."

If the rebel still balks, well ... here's a firm, clear, but still polite response:

"John, 100% board giving is required at many of the foundations we want to ask for grants. I understand that you have some questions and reservations, but those reservations are potentially jeopardizing thousands or tens of thousands of dollars that could come to the Historical Society, and that's really troublesome."

If your rebel isn't willing to give at least $20 after hearing that ... well, I believe it's time for hardball. Giving to the nonprofit is such an essential duty of a board member that if a "rebel" board member still isn't willing to give, then the board chair should seriously consider whether that member should be on the board. I'm serious, this is a big deal. If a board member is being a pain about this basic responsibility, *he or she shouldn't be on the board.*

"John, I believe you are putting your own personal feelings ahead of the welfare of the Historical Society. That's a serious problem and violates your duty as a board member. I'd like you to reconsider why you're on the board in the first place." At that point, I would advise not taking a gift and letting John stew on it for a day or two.

This is a *very* heavy-handed approach. But I've come to believe you've got to fight on this one. Giving is a basic responsibility, and there should be no excuses.

You will probably never get to the final arguments with any rebel board member. In a small meeting, without a crowd to grandstand in front of, your rebel is much more likely to go with the flow ... just don't count on it.

ONE CAVEAT

I'm already qualifying myself, but there are a few select situations where a board member may have a valid excuse for not giving. Poverty is one.

In most scenarios, someone impoverished probably won't be on your board, but a nonprofit dealing with poverty might find it appropriate to have a member of the population it serves sitting on the board. This person shouldn't be required to give.

And a vow of poverty is another exception—don't expect priests or nuns to give. They might give, but they shouldn't be required to. In these instances, you can have a board member give on behalf of the non-donor member and by any reasonable measure still have 100% board participation.

DEALING WITH A WEAK BOARD CHAIR

Since dealing with the rebel involved a board chair willing to go to the mat for you and the organization, we may as well immediately jump to the problem of a weak board chair.

Afraid of arguments on the board, afraid of being seen as "mean," afraid of standing up for the executive director ... a weak board chair can be death.

Whenever you get a new board chair, you need to quickly build a good working relationship. Plan on weekly or biweekly breakfast meetings, regular phone calls and emails, and the like. More than anything, you need to establish mutual trust. You need to be able to trust that the board chair is representing the best interests of the nonprofit *and you.* Your board chair should be your best liaison. The board chair must trust your understanding, dedication, and decision-making. The two of you are a team. Squabbles should be settled privately with a united front to staff and board members.

But if you don't have that, and don't feel that you could successfully create that kind of relationship, then you need to consider other options.

Start with steps outlined above. If you get resistance from the chair on personal giving, calling other board members, or going to more meetings, you're going to need a backup. Suggest that with the importance of fundraising, another board member could be a sort of board cheerleader for this process and get people excited, interested, and giving.

Don't suggest a fundraising committee! We're trying to prevent you from wasting your time, remember? But a cheerleader—someone who you think would have the time and the interest in helping to raise money—is a different thing altogether. Essentially you're just replacing your board chair with someone who actually is willing to work and take a stand. This person doesn't need a formal title. In fact, floating it to the board chair as a "cheerleader" might help you in your cause, since the word sounds vague, not very important, and temporary.

That cheerleader, if you can swing it, should be your next board chair. After your successful fundraising activities, take the person out for a drink to celebrate and float the idea.

If you don't think that you can find someone else to be a champion of board giving, or if your board chair doesn't go for it, you need to get a little bit stronger with your board chair and see if he or she will bend.

"I am worried because without being able to launch a successful fundraising campaign this year, programs may get cut and I might have to consider cutting staff hours. We've got so much potential here. The board seemed interested at the meeting. I just need you to make a few calls and come to a coffee meeting or two. After we get through this month, things will quiet down a lot."

Note that I mentioned working around the board chair before confronting them a little more directly. I am assuming that you—like many of us—would have difficulty getting a little confrontational with your boss and would prefer the work-around solution. But a word of caution: You can't use a work-around solution for everything. It might help you get 100% board giving, but you've got a lot of other things you need your board chair to back you on. If you're not willing to stridently make your case, it's going to be a bad year. Or two years. Or three, depending on how long the chair can keep the position.

The work-around is probably the simplest short-term solution. Asserting yourself, your ideas, and the needs of the organization clearly may pay off better in the long run.

DEALING WITH FOUNDING BOARD MEMBERS

Often some of the volunteers who founded the board are still on it. You might feel it's time for the nonprofit to do new and exciting things, but that the founders are always a stick in the mud about change.

This can make an ask difficult. You want the board member to feel that their input and experience is valuable (and, really, despite the frustration they might cause, they are valuable).

I think the easiest way is to elevate the discussion above the minutiae of the organization. Like dealing with the rebel, go "big picture" and praise the board member's dedication to the organization and the mission that transcends any of the smaller differences you've had with them (or that they've had with other board members).

DEALING WITH BOARD MEMBERS SCARED OF CREDIT CARDS AND TECHNOLOGY

It's possible you might get someone who, on principle, doesn't like that you are taking credit cards because your organization shouldn't be encouraging people to go into debt. They also might object to the fees.

For the first argument, be sure point out that debit cards are just like checkbooks and are a very common payment method. As you try to add new donors to your ranks, you want them to be able to give in the way that feels most comfortable to them. If you need to go on, you could add that your nonprofit can't make people's decisions for them: it's their choice to give and it's their choice how to pay. *Most* credit card users don't have problems with credit and this option should be available to them.

For the second worry about fees, stick with the argument that you expect to receive gifts that wouldn't be possible without credit cards, especially at annual events like auctions.

For people worried about the privacy of their card numbers, you need to make sure they understand how seriously you take the responsibility of having a number on file. *And do take it seriously!* In an age of identity theft, this is essential. Access to those numbers should be limited to no more than two people. If you don't have a safe, buy a small fireproof lockbox. Only you and the bookkeeper should have a key. And set a policy that you process the cards only when you're both in the office. You should be aware whenever those numbers aren't locked up.

DEALING WITH THE BOARD MEMBER WHO IS A GOOD GIVER

In some ways, the person who has already written the check for $250, or $1,000, or $5,000 is the hardest person you'll approach for money.

Do you ask for more, do you ask for the same, do you even name a number at all?

First, bring your board chair along. You want to make sure this donor knows how appreciated their gift is.

Second, for this donor, you should do a little more research. Look back through your files—databases, bookkeeping software, old annual reports, whatever you have—and try to track this board member's giving history. How much have they given annually? Can you tell how they gave? (For example, did they buy an expensive item at an auction or give over the phone?)

You want to know as much as you can about their giving.

If their last gift was within your current fiscal year, then you shouldn't be aiming to get a lot out of them. You might want to show them how much their last gift was, when it was made, and ask for a "token amount" as part of this current board campaign. But you should plan on sitting down with them again around the anniversary of their last gift.

Alternatively, you could simply sit down and get to know one of your best donors. Since they gave in your current fiscal year, you don't need the gift to get to your goal of 100% board giving. They've already given it. So you could take the time to ask them questions and learn about why they like your organization so much. It will help you learn about what donors are looking for, but also give you valuable insight into asking this person for a gift next year.

If the board member's last gift falls outside your current fiscal year, then still take the chance to get to know them and thank them for their last gift.

When you get to the ask, keep it simple. "Your generosity really made an impact and I hope you might be able to make a similar gift again this year."

Or: "With so many on the board stepping up, we have a lot of potential this year working together. Would you be able to consider a gift of $350 toward our goal?" (You can also suggest something like $30/month instead of a flat amount.)

For this donor, $350 would be an increase of $100. If you want to try for a larger gift, consider previous years of giving: if they've given $250 a couple of years in a row, then you should feel better about asking for an increase. But don't try to double their previous gift just yet.

Again, once you've made the ask, sit quietly and let them think about it. It's their move now, and an uncomfortable silence is not your job to fill. Sip your water or your coffee, and wait for their response. And then thank them for whatever they decide!

NEW BOARD MEMBERS

Now that you have 100% of the board giving, be sure that this information is conveyed to potential prospects for the board. Boards frequently interview potential candidates. You don't want to ask, "Would it be a problem to give X amount?" But you can tell candidates that board members are expected to give "time, talent, and treasure," and tell them how proud you were that 100% of the current board gave, at X amount, with an average gift of Y. You may be able to tell from their reaction whether they could make a similar gift.

Don't be taken in by board members who say that they are committed to raising a certain amount from other people even if they can't give on their own. Board members should be a part of fundraising anyway. It's not an either/or proposition.

There are a million things to look for in a potential board member, of course. A belief in the mission, experience on a board, and a sound temperament are pretty high on the list. But ideally your board should grow wealthier as its members get replaced. As you start meeting donors over the next year, look for those who have a real passion for your organization. Get them involved in a small way as a volunteer on a committee or at an event. Later, if someone seems like a good fit, you can suggest they join. Board members should be doing the same thing.

ONE YEAR LATER: THE 10% INCREASE NO ONE FEELS

Thanks to your new ability to run recurring gifts on stored credit cards, your next ask a year later is going to be a much quicker process.

I recommend a phone call for the second ask. Thank the board member again for their donation. Tell them that you'd like to keep a recurring gift going for them during the next year so the board can keep its 100% giving goal. And ask if they would consider giving X dollars per month. If they were giving $10, suggest $15. If they were giving

$30, suggest $40. If they were giving $50, suggest $60. If $100, suggest $110 or maybe even $120.

Note that on a percentage basis, the suggested increases go down. An increase from $10 to $15 is a 50% increase, but it's only a total of $60 more. An increase from $100 to $110 is a 10% increase, but you're getting $120 more annually. Aim for a 10% increase for larger donors. For smaller monthly gifts like $10 to $50/month, you can ask for more and likely get it.

Most donors won't notice the difference.

AND FINALLY: EXPIRING CREDIT CARDS

Every month you run the numbers, make sure your bookkeeper is paying attention to expiration dates. Within a month of the expiration you'll want to call the donor and get a new card. Don't wait till the end. You'll want to leave yourself time to get the card rolled over.

COUNTERPOINT

Each chapter will end with a short counterpoint, so that you can get a sense of some of the nuance with fundraising. The main counterpoint here is to call out that 'good governance' of nonprofits would suggest that the executive director is not the one to ask for money from the board. That job normally falls to a board member itself.

This is true. But it's often … incomplete. Good governance sometimes doesn't match up with the practicalities and culture of small nonprofits. In some small nonprofits, there would be nothing unusual about an executive director asking board members for their annual donation. In others, it would be a real breach of the culture of the organization and might land the executive director in hot water.

Whatever your nonprofit's culture is, find someone to go through these steps with you. It could be the board chair or a "board cheerleader." Loan them this book. Show them the numbers you've collected. You don't want to do this one halfway.

And even if culturally you shouldn't be the one asking for money, ask to go along so you can "practice."

CHAPTER 3

—m—

Asking Outside the Board

A SKING THE PUBLIC for money may sound like a scary endeavor. But it's important to realize that you almost never just ask "the public." You're asking the community of friends who already know about you, already like you, and have already given you contact information.

It's a serious mistake to try to introduce people to your organization at the same time you make an ask. Don't be tempted to paper the town asking for support. Stick with those you know and who already like your organization.

Now, if you are focusing only on people who already know and like your organization, you can easily see the handicaps of being a small nonprofit. Likely, you don't know a lot of people compared to colleges, that can tap alumni and parents, or hospitals, that can look to former patients and families of patients. Even theaters and arts organizations have a certain benefit over other nonprofits because they can turn to their patrons.

Turning back to Linda at the Smallville Historical Society, she knew she had 4,000 people visit the Pioneer Cabin in the previous 12 months. But most left no record, which was—for fundraising purposes at least—about as helpful as if none had come through.

Her list of people interested in the Historical Society was only about 800 people long. Some she had email addresses for, but no home address. Some, vice versa. And some she suspected were long out of date. The information was also stored haphazardly on sheets of paper, in old Excel files, and in a hanging folder system a volunteer had started but never finished.

The idea of going through everything and trying to sort it out was daunting.

At the same time, Linda felt oddly comforted. After all, the Historical

Society was virtually starting from the bottom rung of the development ladder. Its fundraising had been in fits and starts with little to no planning and poor communication with donors. Linda couldn't possibly do worse! A bad year of fundraising wouldn't jeopardize anything because they'd never had a good year of fundraising.

Linda imagined the worst-case scenario she could think of: accidentally insulting a big donor and losing their gift. She wouldn't like it, but at most that meant Linda losing a gift of a few hundred dollars, since they'd never gotten anything larger than that.

The worst-case scenarios Linda came up with didn't threaten the organization financially because there just wasn't a lot to threaten. This made Linda feel more confident as she moved forward.

BE SCRUPULOUS

The Historical Society was liked and respected—among the few in town who knew about it—and Linda wanted to keep it that way. She vowed to fundraise as ethically as she could.

And what was not to like? The society didn't have any scandals, they didn't come with any baggage ... most people saw a group of volunteers and low-paid staff just trying to preserve a small piece of history.

I should say here that you may believe your nonprofit doesn't have a good reputation in the community because of internal strife like board machinations and frustrated staff. Know that this generally doesn't affect an outsider's perception of a nonprofit. It might feel like it from inside the bubble. But most people don't notice or care. It is not unusual to find that the general public feels better about a nonprofit than the organization's own board, simply because the board knows how grueling this past year's budget fight was.

For nonprofits that are involved in controversial or political issues where a large percentage of the population may directly oppose your mission, you may not be universally liked. Don't sweat it. The key is to make sure you are well-liked and respected by the percentage of the population who believes wholeheartedly in your mission. That's the group you want to keep your reputation with, because that's the group where you will find your donors. The same is true of religious organizations. If you run a Catholic rescue mission, you certainly want as broad a swath of the public to respect you as possible, but you should make sure that Catholics really like you.

Giving to Success

Linda was wary of portraying her organization as small and beleaguered, fighting for its survival. She didn't want donors to pity her, she wanted them to be so inspired by the Historical Society that they couldn't help but open their wallets.

It's what donors want, too. They want to give to a successful organization, an organization that has shown it can do good with the dollars it gets.

Consider that there are more than one million 501(c)(3) nonprofits in the United States. In many ways you are in competition with every one of them for your donor's gift. Yes, it's unlikely a donor is choosing between your nonprofit and a food bank in a town they've never heard of. But think about your own charitable gifts.

More than likely you've given to a nonprofit outside your direct region, maybe an out-of-state college or a hometown cause you still believe in. Did you give to the Red Cross after 9/11? Or to them after the tsunami in Japan or Hurricane Katrina? Maybe you support Wikipedia or Heifer International or Greenpeace.

Donors give to organizations that do good—however they define "good"—regardless of their location. They want to see their money go to an organization that is going to use it well, that is successful in its mission. If Wikipedia wasn't such a good resource, no one would give it money. If Heifer didn't get livestock into the hands of the poorest people, no one would give to it. If the Smallville Historical Society didn't educate Smallville about its pioneer history, why would anyone give to it?

Donors don't want to pity you. Show them what you do, show them how it's important, and ask them to support it.

You Only Get To Be Saved Once

Hopefully that heading speaks for itself. Your donors will probably bail you out if you need their help. But don't count on them to do it again. Don't send out dire warnings about how your organization is going to fold if you don't raise $10,000 by the end of the month. Don't scare your donors. If they think there's a chance that their money is going to go to waste—that is, that you really might not make it—then they're going to be that much more wary about giving.

Certainly some who truly love you will rally to your side if they hear you might have to shutter your doors. But if they're that dedicated, they'll give without the threat of your extinction, too.

Of course, if you really *do* need to be saved, then by all means go out and ask to be saved. Get out of the danger zone. Ideally, you should have a plan approved by the board and formed with input from your donors and the people you serve that lays out a plan for the future so that you can explain to the public why you're not going to need to be saved again.

ASKING

Now that we've covered some basic "big picture" concepts for asking for money, we have to tackle the practicalities. How do you go about raising money?

First, avoid the temptation to throw an event! We'll deal with events in the next section. But for now, know that most fundraising events take many hours of work for not nearly enough money. Remember, Linda earned more than $100/hour for the Historical Society doing her direct asks. We want to identify fundraising activities that can produce results as close to that as possible.

This is the next step of the development plan for the year: going outside the board of directors and asking for money from your nonprofit's friends.

We're going to choose the most basic tool for a fundraiser: a mailing.

HOW TO PLAN AHEAD FOR A MAILING

It's easy to think, "Hey, a mailing! Piece of cake!" If you've tried one before, you know that's not the case. Mailings are all about attention to detail; stay on top of the details and you'll do fine. Plan ahead and you can get through yours painlessly.

As a first planning note: if you have a handful of major donors--for our purposes, let's call "major donors" those that give 5 to 10 times your average gift size—then make your ask of these donors first, in as personal a way as you can. You don't want to include them in a direct mail campaign like this! Solicit a gift from them using the recommendations in Chapter 5 before you spend time on the mailing.

If you don't have at least five "major donors," then a mailing like this is one of the better ways to identify potential big givers. But again: exclude any major donors from this mailing. They deserve a more personal ask.

Here's the big picture for a direct mail campaign: if you're sending a mailing to people who have already self-identified (as in, given you their address), then you should expect a return of somewhere between 5% and 10%. So if you send out 1,000 letters, a safe budget would be for about 50 responses.

But how can you budget when you don't know what people will give? If your organization hasn't run a mailing before, you can't do anything better than a good guess. The best way to make that guess is to take your average gift for the last year (which you calculated for the board in Section I) and increase it by $10 to $20. So if your average gift was $40, budgeting for a $50 or $60 return is probably in the ballpark. (We'll get to how we're going to increase that average gift size in a bit.)

So, if you send out 1,000 letters, and you're expecting an average gift size of $50, you should expect to bring in $2,500 (50 donors x $50).

But of course it's going to cost something to send out those letters ...

- The cost of envelopes.

- The cost of the paper (1,000 letters is two reams of paper if the letter is one page long, and four reams of paper if the letter is two pages long) for the letter and a couple hundred sheets for the reply cards. Will cost extra if you have to print the letterhead, too.

- The cost of return envelopes.

- The cost of postage.

Costs for all of this are going to vary, but there's one thing that will always be true: the more you buy, the less it costs.

With all that printing, look for a printer that will print everything above that you don't have already and run a mail-merged document for you. Is it going to cost more than if you run it all from your office printer? Most definitely. But it's usually worth it.

TO STUFF OR NOT TO STUFF?

You might be tempted to have an envelope stuffing party with a couple of volunteers, and for batches under a few thousand it's the best way to go. Four people can spend a few hours stuffing for the cost of a pizza.

If you have more names than that, you may want to find a mail house that can stuff and send everything for you.

POSTAGE

All organizations and businesses get discounts on postage for sending bulk mailings. Nonprofits can get bigger discounts by signing up for a nonprofit rate at the post office. If your organization doesn't have an account with the post office, this website has a good step-by-step guide for setting up that account: **http://bit.ly/nonprofitpostage.**

For now, don't worry about giving your donors business reply envelopes, either. (These are the envelopes that don't cost your donor any postage because you pick it up.) This is an expense that's not worth it yet for the number of gifts you're going to be bringing in.

Your costs shouldn't be more than $1/letter and ideally should be much less than that—which gets easier as your database grows. So if you had a total cost of $1.00/letter to mail that brought in $2,500, you would be budgeting to make at least $1,500 after expenses.

Now, most likely you're actually going to make more than that. In fact, we're hoping that instead of mostly small gifts, this letter will earn some larger gifts as well, bringing the total up at least another $1,000. The real hope is to spend less than 25 cents for every dollar raised on a mailing like this. So if your costs are $1,000, you'd want to raise $4,000.

But don't worry if you don't get there on your first mailing! It's hard to budget for that when your database is small and you've never attempted an ask like this before. It's also important to realize that every organization has a variety of factors—from location to mission—that dramatically affect the cost per dollar raised. Spending a quarter or less per dollar raised is a good goal (20 cents is actually the national average), but specific circumstances may prevent your organization from raising money at that rate.

The main reason for the exercise above is to make sure you have a good baseline. If your average gift was too small and your costs too high, then this estimating process would tell you that you need to move as much of the operation in-house as possible to save costs or drop the idea of a mailing and instead do a phone-a-thon (more on that at the end of this chapter), which takes more labor but has less material costs.

BACK TO YOUR DATABASE

Linda wasn't sure where to begin. She had a list of donors from the last year that she'd pulled from records. Everything before that was not as reliable. At the very least, she knew that every name she had was because someone had been interested enough in the Historical Society to give their information. Linda turned over all the records she had found to her bookkeeper and asked her to input everything into the standard format she had created in her new database.

Names should be entered as close as possible to the way they were given to you. For example, if someone writes, "Mr. and Mrs. David Smith," then that's how your letter should begin, and your database should know that. On the sample database online there is a field for First Names, Last Name, and Salutation. This allows you to keep track of Mrs. Smith's first name, while also mailing it to their preferred salutation. Names can be a lightning rod issue for many people, and you never want to make assumptions.

While her bookkeeper worked on that, Linda called around to a couple of mail houses in her area. Once she found someone she liked, Linda sent them the finished database of names. The mail house went through all the names and addresses and scrubbed it for bad addresses. This is a valuable service and should be done once a year to make sure you're not spending money mailing to people who have moved.

WRITING THE LETTER

A solicitation letter is an unusual form of writing. There are many ways to do it, and all have certain benefits. There are many books about writing a good solicitation letter based on studies of response rates to different styles of letters. For example, letters longer than two pages tend to have better responses.

I won't argue with the good data of the researchers, but I will say this: unless you have a very large database of names, most of these factors probably won't affect your return in any meaningful way. The most important point for you is to craft an honest, well-written letter that clearly makes a case for giving.

For now, *just get the letter written.* If you have run regular annual **appeals** in the past, and you have a large database of donors, spending the time to learn and apply this information will probably help you get more out of your letters.

If you are just starting out ... well, it's an overused expression, but the perfect is the enemy of the good. Spending a lot of hours now researching the perfect letter will just delay you. Let's just get this first year's mailing out the door.

You can find a sample ask letter online at **www.thelittlebookofgold. com/index.php/downloads**. In addition, I recommend keeping a file of all the solicitation letters you get. Pay attention to the letters that inspire you to give.

When I sit down to write a solicitation letter, I have a structure in my mind. I'll walk you through the process.

STEP 1: DEFINE YOUR PITCH

Before you start writing, you need to know what you're aiming for. I like to draft my "topic" sentence. It's not the first sentence of the letter—most likely it will be at the end of the first or second paragraph. But this is the key sentence. When you write that first paragraph or two, this is the sentence you will be aiming for.

"Your support will help us keep the museum at the center of the Rochester art community."

"Giving to the Smallville County AIDS Foundation means we can increase our education and outreach as part of our effort to stop the spread of AIDS in our county."

"Your gift will go directly toward serving the children of our community through after-school enrichment with dedicated tutors."

Note that each sentence puts the organization in context with something bigger than itself. The goal you present donors is to help the arts, stop the spread of AIDS, or tutor children. The nonprofit is only a conduit for that goal.

STEP 2: START YOUR LETTER OFF RIGHT

First things first: Write "Dear ***," on the first line. Those three asterisks will remind you and the printer that this letter needs to be mail-merged with your database. Don't write, "Dear Melissa," and expect you'll remember to change it later. You're likely to end up printing 1,000 letters that all begin "Dear Melissa."

Now that you've identified what you want your donors to give toward, you need to begin writing your letter aimed at that goal. Here are some ideas to get you started ...

- Cite a positive quote from a news source or a prominent person in your community.

- Share a success story about someone you serve (but remember to get permission first!).

- Share a donor's story about why they feel good giving to your organization.

- Redefine your organization. ("Most people think of us as just a pioneer cabin. But what they don't see is the work we do helping residents trace their family lines, educating kids on the importance of history, and building stronger community bonds.")

- Or simply re-introduce yourself ("For the last 10 years, the Smallville Historical Society has worked to inspire the people of Smallville to engage with the history of our great town").

Use no more than a paragraph or two to get to your thesis sentence above. Don't fall into the temptation to hold off until the end. Donors need to know the reason for the letter early on. It's not a secret.

STEP 3: ANSWER THE BIG QUESTION: WHY SHOULD I CARE?

Once you've started your letter and made your ask, the next task is to flesh it out a little more. This should take two to four paragraphs. Here you want to expand on two themes: the importance of the need, and why your organization is the one to fill that need.

So ... what's the need? Well, we've already started to address that. The need is going to be pretty synonymous with your mission, or very closely related. It's not about you, it's about the people you serve.

This can be a good place for statistics ("According to recent research, children who receive after-school tutoring are 10 times more likely to ...").

As you start this section of the letter, consider what came ahead of it. The sentence just before ended something like "... help us keep the museum at the center of the Rochester art community." Now is the time to get more specific. Do you want to write about students who need art enrichment? Artists who need to be recognized? The community that needs the opportunity to see art?

Each may be equally valid. It's up to you to know which will "sell" to your donors.

There are some ways you might be able to figure out what they will like. You could ask a couple of board members what they like best about your organization. You could base your decision on information you already have about the popularity of certain programs. You could also send one letter to half your database and one to the other and see which gets the better response (this works best if you have a large database).

Or you could just go with your gut—I'm always a fan of the gut decision. You might try to think which program could you see as a 30-second feature on the local news. If it can play well on TV, it will probably play well in your letter.

Now that you've expanded on the need, turn to your organization. If you talked about how much students need art in their lives, then describe how your art classes help fill that need. If you talked about the plight of people living with AIDS, then talk about how important your education outreach is to stopping the spread of the disease. This is the place to talk up your organization.

STEP 4: THE GIFT

It's time to get back to the gift. After talking up your organization, you have a good lead-in for talking about the gift you want your donor to make.

You've probably seen this often. "A gift of just $65 means another student gets after-school help for a month. A gift of $150 provides a year of new textbooks to a struggling student who can't afford her own.

And a gift of $550 provides hands-on summer enrichment so students don't fall behind." And so on.

This is an effective way to set out some levels. But it comes with a couple perils.

First, make sure that your levels sound reasonable. Writing "$70 buys the library a new textbook" will make everyone think, "Why is the library paying so much for textbooks?" Even if there's a good answer, you don't want to raise the question.

Second, don't handicap yourself by aiming too low. Writing "$15 buys art supplies for a student" might be true, but it's also a good way to get a lot of $15 gifts. The minimum amount you call out should be larger than your median gift. For the Historical Society, Linda's most common gift was $20. Asking for $40 or so means she could increase some of those gifts by as much as 100%, giving her a higher average gift overall.

Some experts suggest specific numbers (as in, "$42.58 buys ...") when doing this because they're more believable. In this matter, I really don't have a strong opinion. Does asking for $42.58 mean you get an extra $2.58 from someone who would have given $40 or does it mean you get $2.42 less from someone who would have given $45? I don't know if anyone can answer this question for sure. But in a solicitation letter, this kind of stuff probably won't matter too much.

STEP 5: WRAP IT UP

Ending the letter is actually the easiest part. Just thank your donor.

- "Thank you for considering a gift to the Historical Society."

- "Thank you for considering a gift in support of AIDS education and outreach."

It's also not a bad idea to write something along the lines of, "If you have any questions about the programs of the museum, please don't hesitate to call me."

STEP 6: THE SIGNATURE

A signature from the executive director is never bad, but a signature from the board chair is probably better. Write the letter yourself, have a friendly set of eyes edit it, and then take it to your chair for approval (hopefully just for approval and not for revising).

If you have the technology and the know-how, get the chair to sign a blank piece of paper a couple times with a good pen. Scan the best image into your computer and then insert it into the document.

STEP 7: POST SCRIPT

A "PS" message is a good way to fit in a final reminder and *call to action*.

- "PS—The Historical Society now accepts recurring gifts via credit and debit card! It's a great way to spread your gift out over the year."

- "PS—We're hosting a special cast party for all donors who give more than $100. We hope to see you there!"

THE REPLY CARD

For your reply card, the easiest method is to design it in Word. Like the ask letter, you can find a sample reply card online. That said, getting a professional-looking reply card designed and printed can really help make the sell. Either way, the basic elements should include:

- A place for the donor's name. This is a good place to ask the donor to write how they would like to be recognized for their gift. Generally speaking, the way they would like to be recognized is how you should address future asks.

- A place for the donor to select the amount they would like to give.

- Because you are already running credit cards once a month, you should offer your donors the same option. Include a line that says, "I would like to make a gift of $____ monthly."

- You'll also want to include which credit cards you accept.

- Below that, give a place for the name on the credit card, the credit card number, and the expiration date. Check to see if your credit card processor requires the three-digit code on the back or a billing zip code.

PUT IT ALL TOGETHER

You now have all the basic elements. If you have a printer to put everything together, send it all along, including the scrubbed database from a mail house. If you are doing your own stuffing, then at this point you'll be running a mail merge on your office computer and running all your envelopes and solicitation letters through it, followed by a stuffing party.

Once It's Out the Door ... The Thanks

You were probably expecting a little bit of a lull, but there's still work to be done. You still need to get a thank you note created. Get a lot! One thing you want to be doing a lot more of than you used to is thanking people.

You can get a little creative here. At the Grand Cinema, we cut up film from movie trailers and slipped a few inches of it through slits in the thank you card. The thank you card was preprinted with some information about the film itself (what the sprockets were for, how the sound was stored) on one side and just the words "thank you" on the other. By not writing "thank you for your gift," we could use the notes for volunteers or other purposes.

Our thank you cards were interesting, in line with our mission, and—best of all!—relatively cheap, since we had a virtually unlimited supply of film.

There might be something linked to your organization that would be similar. If it's an interesting enough card, donors might set it out or put it on their refrigerator.

Thank you notes shouldn't necessarily replace thank you letters, however. You should write a short thank you letter that re-emphasizes the themes of the letter. Print it on letterhead and slip your thank you note in to the envelope with it.

The key here is that under the letter you should write, "This letter serves as a receipt for a donation of $*** to the Smallville Historical Society" so that the donor can save have a record for taxes. (For donors who give more than $50 in a calendar year—and especially for donors who make recurring gifts—you should also send a receipt for all gifts made in the year so that they have the appropriate tax information by January 31.)

Have the letter and note ready to go as soon as the mailings go out the door. You'll want to respond within a week at most, though two days is even better.

Remember, too, that Linda had asked board members to call and thank donors who gave more than $50. As donations came in, she forwarded phone numbers (whenever she had them) to board members via email for them to call.

TIMELINE

If you are aiming to get your mailing out to donors by a certain time—say, the end of the year, as was Linda's goal—then you should have a sense of how long this process will take.

- **Early October:** Bookkeeper started work on the database. Linda found a printer for stationery and envelopes.

- **Mid-October:** Linda wrote the letter and sent the completed database to a mail house.

- **Late October:** Linda showed the letter to a friend and her board chair and got a final version approved.

- **Early November:** Linda created a reply card and sent it, the scrubbed database, and the letter to the printer who had already completed the stationery and envelopes.

- **Mid-November:** The printer completed everything and sent the completed letters to the mail house.

- **Late November:** The mail house got the letters out.

- **Early December:** Because the letters were sent using the nonprofit rate, they sat for a week before the post office mailed them. Donors didn't get the letters until December 8.

If you have to do all your printing, then you should expect ten to twelve weeks. If you already have the envelopes and stationery done and your database doesn't need to be created from scratch, you can get a mailing out in less than two months, though two months is still the safest bet.

WRAP-UP

When the donations started to come back in, Linda was overwhelmed by the response. She'd budgeted for a 5% return and instead got 10%.

The median gift was $40, the smallest amount she called out in the letter, with a lot of people giving $20 or $25. But there were a small handful who gave $130 and two who gave $260. Board members called everyone who gave $50 or more (a total of about 30 people, which meant that each of the nine board members made three to four calls).

In all, Linda's letter brought in $3,940 at a cost of $1000. Added to the $1,720 she raised from the board and staff, Linda's efforts had secured $5,660 so far.

She added up the time she and the bookkeeper spent on the project: from creating the database to writing the letter to managing the printing and mailing to managing the thank-yous. She estimated about 40 hours of work over three months, which meant that they'd raised $98.50 per hour, almost exactly the same rate she'd made from the board. (Eventually, time invested in "major gift" asks will be much more lucrative than time invested in mailings. But since Linda was only asking for a few hundred dollars at most from her board members for their first time out, the per hour rate wasn't as high as it could be.)

Linda also decided that in May she would send another letter to everyone on the list who didn't give. If 10% gave on the first letter, she figured that she could probably get 5% on the second mailing.

SOME NOTES ABOUT DONOR RESPONSES

While the mailing was a success, Linda did get her share of cranky phone calls. Despite her best efforts, she heard from callers who were upset about how the letter was addressed, callers upset that they were being asked for money and wanted to be taken off the list, and a volunteer who was insulted that for all the time she'd given to the Historical Society she would still be asked for money.

Linda didn't worry too much about the first calls. She figured she was bound to hit some people who didn't want to get her mailings, and with so many names written down before she even started at the Historical Society, it would have been surprising if they'd gotten no calls from people who had changed their name in the meantime. Most people can handle this and when they called they were very friendly about the change. But some people have sensitive spots around these issues and will complain. It's just part of fundraising. Linda fixed all the names and asked the people who didn't want to receive mailings if they would still like to get the quarterly newsletter. She added a column to the spreadsheet with a checkbox for those who didn't want to be asked for money but still wanted information.

The last call—the irate volunteer—caught Linda completely off guard. She suddenly worried that she had damaged the Historical Society's relationship with its volunteers by including their names in the mailing.

Not true. Two important points if you are worried about soliciting funds from your volunteers:

1) Volunteers like you. That's why they volunteer with you. If you ask them for money in a professional, ethical way, they are more likely to give than just about anyone. Including them in an appeal is absolutely OK. If they give, thank them personally the next time you see them. If they don't give, it shouldn't come up.

2) You need to treat volunteers—or anyone else for that matter— as grown-ups. Everyone is capable of saying "no" when asked for money, especially when it comes in an appeal as passive as a mailing. People can always turn you down, and when that happens, there should be no guilt trip and they should be thanked for hearing you out.

Some people have significant hang-ups about money. The volunteer who called Linda talked about her financial obligations, how she couldn't be expected to "pay to be a volunteer," and that she gave her time the Historical Society but was now questioning whether she wanted to give even that.

Linda did her best to tell her volunteer she certainly didn't expect a gift from her. She thanked her profusely for her volunteering, hoped she would continue, and asked her if she would like to be removed from mailings in the future.

This kind of call could just as easily come from anyone who received the mailing. They can't be predicted or prevented, only mitigated.

Mail Something That Isn't an Ask

Send donors and non-donors a newsletter. Or an invitation to a lecture.

Ask them to volunteer at "Clean up the Park Day." Whatever it is, include your donors in your mission.

Don't look at this as a chore. It's a chance for people to learn more about what you do or to even lend a hand themselves. It's also a chance for you to get to know your donors and potential donors. Don't approach these opportunities like a door-to-door salesman. Just be yourself. Share your love of your organization with others and you'll start to have a good sense of who shares that same passion.

This is like when we counted how many times you'd "touched" board members before asking them for a gift. The more touches, the higher likelihood you'll get a bigger gift when you ask again.

If you can do those extra touches via email, by all means go for it! Email can save you a lot of money, because the cost of non-fundraising mailings can add up. Even so, the expense is often worth the extra contact.

A side note: there is a school of thought that says you shouldn't send donors any material that doesn't have a reply card in it. I'm not sure this is a good choice for a small nonprofit ramping up its fundraising efforts. Don't hit them over the head too early. You want to create a culture of giving in your donors. You can't do that if you create a culture of asking instead.

THE PHONE-A-THON

Many nonprofits prefer "Phone-A-Thon" nights to a mailing. Because a phone call is more personal than a mailing, it will generally have a higher return rate.

My preference is still for mailings, but we should touch on phone-a-thons.

Phone-a-thons provide a personal touch to donors and can generate higher returns. But they are incredibly labor-intensive. A small phone-a-thon might not take much more time than a mailing. But double the size of your list and things change in a hurry. Phon-a-thons can be stressful for you, because they mean working evening hours.

Large nonprofits often schedule a phone-a-thon a few weeks after a mailing goes out. This gives donors a chance to send in their gift via mail before a phone call. A call can also remind someone that they had been meaning to give. Combined, these are an effective package.

I still want to stress, though, that the labor cost can be substantial. My recommendation would be to use a phone-a-thon for donors who haven't given after two mailings. Or to have a board night of calling and have the board call the highest previous donors on the list who haven't given yet this year.

A phone-a-thon can be an effective tool when used correctly. But for a time-pressed nonprofit manager, I'm a fan of the mailing.

ONE YEAR LATER

The goal for the next year's mailing is two-fold: Increase the number of people on the list, and increase the gift size from those already giving.

Increasing gift sizes can be done by segmenting the letters. For example, everyone who gave in the last year might get a letter asking them to give a recurring gift, with amounts that are larger than those listed on the letters going to people who have never given. Also, the top few donors may be singled out for a phone or face-to-face solicitation from you or a board member. We'll cover those larger gift asks in Chapter 5.

We'll deal with increasing the size of the database in the next chapter. As it happens, it's Linda's goal, too …

COUNTERPOINT

In the long run, I don't know how I feel about mailings and phon-a-thons.

Things like caller ID and cell phones are hurting phon-a-thon responses—many people won't pick up if they don't recognize the number. And who knows what's going to happen with the post office and what that will do to the cost of a mailing?

It is tempting to thing that with these barriers that email or texting communications can be a cheap and easy way to reach donors instead. These tools show promise, but they can't yet replace traditional fundraising methods. Email is hard to get the response rate, and texting is still not widely adopted (and not well geared toward larger gifts).

But it's important that you pay attention to these new opportunities. Test them out on small groups of younger donors and see what works.

If your mailings or phon-a-thons ever start to lose their return, then you'll have some things in the works to replace them.

CHAPTER 4

—⟋⟋⟍—

Events Will Kill You

A s YOU'LL RECALL, we are working outward from a central core of people who are dedicated to your organization and your mission, toward people who are less aware and less dedicated. The goal now is to find as many people as possible that we can pull closer. We also need to find new ways to get donations from those who have already given. This is where events can be important.

But note where events fall in the grand scheme of fundraising. Most events are highly inefficient—you can sink hundreds of hours of your time and volunteers' time into an event and get less out of it than what Linda has raised so far. In the process, they'll take you away from your organization's mission and—worst of all—they'll likely burn you out.

In my experience, most nonprofits don't know how to manage fundraising events effectively. Far too often, "Let's throw a fundraiser!" is the go-to response to raising money. I would even go so far as to say that most fundraising events thrown by small nonprofits *lose money*, often without the nonprofit even realizing it. I'm serious when I say events will kill you.

Event Economics 101

At their base, fundraising events are predicated on the idea that you need to give donors something for their gift other than your sincere appreciation. Depending on the kind of event, you may be giving them public recognition for their gift in front of their peers, a night of dinner and dancing, a tangible item (through an auction, for example), or the thrill of competition on the golf course.

That's not necessarily a bad thing. In fact, this is one of the reasons why events are good at bringing potential donors closer to your organization. A guy who loves any excuse to play golf may participate in a golf tournament benefiting an organization he is barely aware of.

Then that nonprofit has the opportunity to put its message and mission in front of him. If he becomes interested and supports the organization more, then great! If not, he still gave on the golf course.

So what's the problem with events? There are a few, but I'll stick with the biggest: hidden costs.

Staff: The Cost You Don't See

Before Linda started her targeted fundraising, she put in a lot of hours toward the Historical Society's annual auction. It made $2,500 that night. How would we evaluate whether it'd been a success?

The first question would be: how many hours did Linda and her paid staff put into it? In previous sections, Linda tracked her time on various fundraising projects. We need to do the same on events. We want to find out what you're getting out of your event—$50/hour, $20/hour, $10/hour?

Linda estimated she and her staff spent 100 hours on the auction, though she suspected that if she'd been keeping track while she was working on it, instead of estimating afterward, she would have come up with a much higher number. At her 100-hour estimate, that meant the staff had made $25/hour working on the auction.

That wouldn't be so bad if all that work had been for free. Linda added up the cost of her time and the time of her staff and realized that, on average they were paid $15/hour. That meant that the nonprofit had made only $10/hour on the event. *Staff are not free.* Even if they're salaried. Staff costs might not show on your event budget, which takes into account revenue and expenses without staff time, but staff time still has to be accounted for.

Opportunity Cost

Here's the kicker, though—and I'm going to steal from the world of business and economics to explain it. The Historical Society had another cost: *opportunity cost.* Opportunity cost is a business term to describe something we all intuitively know: you can't do two things at once. If you spend $10,000 on a new car, you can't spend the same $10,000 to remodel your bathroom. Not being able to remodel the bathroom is the opportunity cost of getting the new car. Spending your money on one thing prohibits the other.

The same goes for your time. If you spend your weekend catching up on work, you didn't get to spend your weekend on chores around the house.

How does that apply to Linda's auction? The 100 hours Linda spent on the auction was time away from doing something else. Linda and her staff invested 100 hours of time and got just $10/hour back. Think what else they could have done with that time!

With her board appeal and solicitation letter, Linda had made about $85/hour for the Historical Society (that's $100/hour minus her estimate of staff costs). By spending time on an event that netted $10/hour, Linda had passed up the opportunity to net $85/hour.

Linda did not like fundraising. She would much rather spend her time building the programs of the Historical Society. She had big dreams for what the organization could do and she wanted to focus on those. Which meant that every hour she spent away from that should be as effective as possible. If she had to spend time on fundraising, then it was going to be where those hours would be put to the best use. And that certainly wasn't the auction, at least as the numbers stood.

AND YET ...

Linda realized that there probably weren't any options left that would prove to be as profitable as the board appeal and fundraising letter. Whatever she did next likely wouldn't raise as much. But she thought she could do a lot better than $10/hour.

So what could she do? The first option was to retool the auction to be a lot more profitable. Here are some ideas that you might consider as you evaluate the events your nonprofit currently runs.

EVERYONE PAYS

Everyone should pay to come to the event. This is especially true for your board, but it also holds true for even you. Everyone pays. This gets trickier for volunteers, but the goal should be to get volunteers to pay as well. I hope that doesn't sound too Draconian, but it doesn't take that many free meals and free swag to sink the profitability of an event. If you are uncomfortable insisting on this, then set a lower ticket price for staff and volunteers that covers the cost of their food. That said, know that 20 minutes of setup work should not be exchanged for $20 off the ticket price. A volunteer should be willing to work *at least half the event* for a discounted ticket. Still, don't comp if you can help it.

Also, I would recommend against reduced tickets for couples. There is little compelling reason to give couples a break, since your hard costs don't really go down, and most people would prefer to bring a guest anyway.

THE $20 RULE OF EVENTS

This is my own particular rule, but I think you'll find it's true. For a long-running and successful event, you can always add $20 to the ticket price. A popular auction with a ticket price of $40 per person can increase it to $60 and most people will pay the increase without a second thought. You may lose a few people, but the increased rate will more than make up for it.

Note: this rule applies only to events that are already running and popular, where attendance is steady or increasing. And a second note: with expensive events, $100/ticket and up, you can still add the $20, but you'd probably do better to figure out ways to get that extra $20/person at the event instead of in the ticket price.

THE $100 RULE OF EVENTS

This is also a rule of my own making. If your event is charging $100/ticket, then you should be able to raise a significant portion of your budget from business sponsorships. The argument behind this is simple: there are a lot of businesses that would like to get their names in front of couples willing to drop $200 for a fundraising event. For events under $100/ticket, the opportunities aren't as obvious, but possibilities can still be there for events with $60+ prices.

ASK FOR A DONATION IN THE INVITATION

On the reply card for your event, you should include a line like, "I can't attend the auction, but would like to contribute $_____ to its success." A Catholic high school might include a line that reads, "I would like to sponsor ____ priests to attend the auction." This functionally works the same as the first option, but gives you the ability to have people attend who are "sponsored" by someone else. It can work for clergy, but also can work for anyone related to your event who wouldn't otherwise be able to attend.

GET CREDIT CARDS ON FILE EARLY

The reason casinos use chips instead of money is that you don't feel as if you're spending "real" money. "Oh, I'll just bet these two little black chips," you say. But you'd probably think a lot harder about shelling out $200 in cash.

The same theory applies to events. At registration, get credit cards on file for attendees and give them a number. It doesn't need to be an auction, although that's where this practice is normally done. But once people have a number, it's much easier for them to just write it down to pay for raffle tickets, centerpieces, etc. I recommend having as many volunteers as you can to get people through registration so that this process is quick and painless for the donor.

RUN YOUR EVENT LIKE A BANK

You absolutely *must* protect your organization and the donors. I know of two nonprofits that lost thousands of dollars on fundraisers because volunteers working the event pocketed cash. There were no checks and balances on any of the cash or credit cards.

I'm not saying your staff or volunteers are stealing from you. I'm saying that the best way to trust them is to not give them a chance. This isn't about turning operations into a casino cage and treating volunteers like prisoners. But show that you have at least moderate safeguards on handling cash so it's clear to volunteers and staff that someone's paying attention.

For starters, invest in at least two lockboxes for cash to keep it safe on the day of the event. Make sure cash is counted with at least two people present. Shred (or delete) any credit cards you collect from donors who don't become monthly donors. (Note: using credit and debit cards is the best way to keep the amount of cash going through staff and volunteer hands to a minimum—another great benefit of plastic.) Don't pay any vendor with cash you bring in; all that money should be in checks or paid from a separate petty cash fund that only you have access to. Set up a structure to handle money that makes sense to you and you'll eliminate 99.9% of potential problems.

Be Wary of "Donor Cultivation" Events

As tickets to fundraising events start to get more pricey (and also more effective for the organization), they attract fewer new, prospective donors. This, again, is not necessarily a bad thing, because it means you are working with donors already close to you and getting even more contributions from them. But you still need a way to attract new donors.

In response, many large nonprofits will make distinctions between fundraising events and "donor cultivation" events. The term describes an event with a cheap (or free) ticket, with a relatively low cost for the organization. There is usually no ask or perhaps a very soft, passive ask. Instead the goal is getting contact information and networking with attendees.

This model has a few drawbacks when it comes to small nonprofits.

First, no matter how hard you try, it can be difficult to get the addresses you want at donor acquisition events. And if you can't get contact information, you can't cultivate donors afterward, which was pretty much the whole point to begin with.

Second, in my experience this model tends to add too many events to the calendar. Donor cultivation events might be *relatively* cheap and quick to produce versus a major fundraiser, but start having a few of them and the cost adds up quickly, especially when your time is factored in to the event cost.

With that in mind, your free donor acquisition event that brings in $0/hour is costing you whatever your hourly rate is (or would be, if you converted your salary to its hourly rate equivalent). If you make $20/hour and spend 15 hours on a free donor acquisition event, your nonprofit spent $300 to make that event happen before any hard costs were taken into account. For the Historical Society, that would be a cost larger than Linda's largest gift.

It is true that over time, donor acquisition events do pay for themselves and then some. Staff time of $300 is made up over the next few years as the people who came to your event start giving. But most small nonprofits with fledgling fundraising efforts can do better with that staff time. Because of the notoriously high turnover rate at small nonprofits, it's likely that right when the payoff from the cultivation event should be happening, your staff is starting to turn over and you can't follow through as you should. As an organization's fundraising gets more institutionalized and professional, these events make more sense.

The next section deals with a fundraising event that also serves as a donor cultivation event quite well. If you feel the need to bring in prospective donors with an event, my advice would be to make the event as close to your mission as possible involving work you likely already would have done. Also, certain events that cultivates current donors may be appropriate to open to a wider, more public audience.

I don't want to outright say that you shouldn't have donor cultivation events. Just be wary of the dangers.

THE ONE EVENT YOU SHOULD ADD

Considering everything above, you might think that I'm down on all events. Not true! In fact there is one event that I absolutely love. It attracts new donors. It gets big gifts from current donors. It has a low cost to produce and the chance for an incredible "hourly rate."

This wonderful magic event is ... breakfast. That's right, breakfast.

WHY YOU SHOULD LOVE BREAKFAST

Let's go through some of the benefits of breakfast fundraisers. The first benefit is cost. If you've thrown an auction or an evening fundraiser, you know that there is one significant cost that has to be dealt with: alcohol. Either you have to charge enough to cover the cost and raise your ticket price accordingly or you have to charge your donors per drink. And at a fundraiser, if your donors are opening their wallets, it's best that the money is going to you and not the bar tab.

But breakfast has no alcohol!

In addition, breakfast is just plain cheaper. Bacon and eggs with muffins, orange juice, and coffee is cheap when compared with appetizers, salad, bread, and an entree. Costs will differ depending on where you are and what caterer you choose, but you can expect breakfast to be one quarter to one half of what you would pay for an evening meal.

In addition to cost, breakfast has one other important benefit: it's short. People need to go to work and they won't want to linger. Those fundraisers that start at 6:00 p.m. and go till 10:00 p.m. or later? Forget 'em! With breakfast, registration starts at 7:00 am. Breakfast is served at 7:30 am. The program starts at 7:45 and ends by 8:45. Everyone's out the door by 9:00 am.

You can't beat it.

WHY DONORS LOVE BREAKFAST

Let me describe how the breakfast might work from my perspective as a donor.

At 7:30, I showed up at the last minute for the Boy Scouts breakfast. There were at least 70 tables of eight, but many on the fringes looked partially empty. I am a former Boy Scout, but had never thought of giving. Mainly I was there because a friend had volunteered to be a table captain and really wanted to have a full table. He had told me it was a free breakfast, but that a gift would be appropriate.

The emcee of the event was a former Scout and a retired CEO of a local company. He spoke at length about Scouting and then introduced three current Scouts who each spoke for about 10 minutes. I noticed that by this point, most chairs were filled. A lot of arrivals had come in late.

After that, a short video about Scouts played on the big screen set to slightly cheesy music.

Then a Scout made the ask. He listed the benefits of Scouting, talked about what it did for young adults, and asked table captains to pass out forms. Everyone at the table got a form and everyone started filling it out. He asked for way more than I could give, but I wrote my credit card number and gave the most I was comfortable giving. While we were filling the form out, he kept talking about the benefits of Scouting.

Everyone turned their form back in to the table captain who put them in a manila envelope. The emcee got back on the stage, thanked everyone for coming, and that was the end of the event.

My $50 gift was at the low end of the scale. Well-established breakfasts with a good program will have an average gift of at least $100. For about 560 attendees, that's at least $56,000 of income for a very low expenditure.

The event doesn't have to get that many people there to be profitable. Here's a step-by-step guide to getting started.

How to Throw a Breakfast Fundraiser
Step 1: Alert the board!

Linda decided to start with the board. She told them that after their success with the recent fundraising efforts, she thought the auction needed to be retooled to be a better fundraising event. Everyone agreed.

Linda left it at that until the next month. When she came to the next meeting, she proposed that the board change the event to a breakfast fundraiser. She talked about the benefits and told the board that it had the potential to raise a lot more money than the auction. She also pointed out how many auctions there already were in town and that it was hard to find a free weekend night not already booked with a major fundraiser. (This is true in most communities—large organizations with the resources to invest in major auctions have the market cornered.)

She showed them a rough draft of a budget that showed a profit of $10,000—much more than the auction would likely do. (For a budget worksheet for the breakfast fundraiser, check the download section of the website.)

She asked the board to support the change to a breakfast fundraiser. From them, all she asked was that each of them volunteer to be a table captain and each find seven people to come to the breakfast with them (assuming tables of eight, which are easier to fill than a table of 10). She reviewed that there would be no ticket price, but that people should come prepared to be asked for a gift. This makes the job of table captain much easier.

Step 2: Choose a Program

The three basic needs of a breakfast fundraiser are a program, a venue, and attendees. Your first goal is establishing the program and the venue. The order of these depends on what kind of program you want, so let's start with that.

Your organization might lend itself well to having your clients speak—Boy Scouts, youth of any kind, a person suffering from the disease your nonprofit works with, and so on. You may also choose to honor someone—my local chapter of the Red Cross does a heroes breakfast that honors people who have saved lives in the community. Former clients are a possibility too—someone formerly homeless, for example. These kinds of presentations can be put together cheaply and easily. Ideally, you can make your program work with local resources. My only caveat would be that you should approach highly emotional or traumatic subjects with extreme caution. Your breakfast event should not be emotionally draining or depressing.

The next option would be to find a regional or national speaker. The key here is that it should be someone intriguing, someone who sounds interesting to people. An expert on homelessness, while informative, may not necessarily be interesting. A professional athlete who spent time sleeping on the streets in his youth may be. An expert on global warming might be boring. A scientist who lived at the South Pole for two years is more intriguing. A woman who lived in a tree for three years to prevent it from being cut down is even more so.

Generally speaking, aim for people who *did* something, as opposed to people who know something.

Finding this person might take some time and research. Look for an athlete, musician, author, or actor who is passionate about your cause, or something broader (they may not be passionate about theater, but they support the arts; they may not be passionate about fighting homelessness but they support civic participation in communities).

More than just online research, look to your friends. Does a friend of a friend know someone famous? And keep your ears open! My second grade teacher's sister was married to a famous actor. What famous people came from your area? Just hearing a famous person talk about growing up in your town will appeal to a lot of people.

If you go with a speaker, it will often mean you'll have to pay a fee that goes either directly to the speaker or to a charity of their choice. That's the main reason why a more personal event is probably better. A recognizable speaker may be able to fill more seats, but you probably won't end up with a dramatically higher profit.

For her program, Linda found a well-spoken high school student who had recently created a school drama project on a Smallville pioneer and had used the resources of the Historical Society extensively. Linda asked him to perform at the breakfast in his costume as a pioneer. She also booked a local prominent architect who had restored a Masonic temple, and asked him to speak on the importance of local history and tracing roots. She paid the high school student $100 for his 10-minute monologue and negotiated to pay the architect $500 for a 20-minute speech and PowerPoint presentation.

STEP 3: THE VENUE
If you have to book a speaker instead of creating your own program, it's not a bad idea to book the speaker before you have a venue. This is especially true if you're aiming for a big name—an athlete or an actor, for example.

If that's not a worry, you can book the venue while you are also working on assembling the program. Aim for a venue that can hold 200 to 250 people seated at tables—that's 25 to 30 tables, plus the stage area. Try to find a place that will comp you the venue in exchange for the catering bill. Don't go too expensive on any of this. You don't need a view or a fancy new convention center. Focus more on the size of the space and the quality of the food—but even then, don't worry too much about the food.

Linda found a venue that could cater a breakfast for 200 for less than $9/person. She also paid them to set up the podium, microphone, and a large screen behind the speaker for the architect's presentation.

STEP 4: FINDING ATTENDEES
With 25 tables, and the board already serving as nine table captains, Linda needed to find sixteen more. She started calling volunteers, former board members, and a few friends and talked up the breakfast. Five people said they would be table captains, and another five said they would like to come.

Then Linda turned to the donor list from her mailing. She'd noted who had a lot of passion for the Historical Society. It wasn't correlated with the gift size, but she recognized some names from the logbook at the Pioneer Cabin; others had scribbled notes saying how much they loved the Historical Society.

Linda called or emailed them, letting them know about the event and also indicating that she was looking for table captains to fill some tables and wondered if they or anyone they knew might be interested. For those who asked what was involved, Linda emailed a one-page document she'd created with tips for being a table captain (available online as well). She got another four table captains, putting her at 18 total captains.

Linda emailed the board news of her success and asked if they knew of someone who might want to be a table captain or who thought they could fill a second table on their own. That got her another three tables, getting her to 21. She called it good for now. With 21 people working to fill tables, she was already expecting at least 150 people, and she hadn't yet sent an invitation.

STEP 5: CREATE AND MAIL AN INVITATION

Linda's invitation was a simple folded card. She had an old black and white picture of the historic Pioneer Cabin printed on the front of the card and ordered enough for a few mailings. Inside she had printed an invitation to the breakfast, with information about the speakers. The invitation made it clear that the event would benefit the Historical Society, but also let people know that admission was free. She asked for RSVPs to be sent in two weeks before. Instead of a reply card, Linda gave her office phone and email address.

STEP 6: PROCESS RSVPS

As RSVPs started to come in, she kept track of them in a separate Excel spreadsheet but also recorded a line in the donor database. Every couple of days she sent a list of new names to the board to make sure that she wasn't recording people twice (someone who had been invited by a board member but also RSVP'd to her).

For people who RSVP'd and didn't have an assigned table, Linda checked to see if they had given to the mailing. A small handful had not only given but had also given enough to warrant a call from a board member. For those, she immediately let that board member know she was seating the donor at their table. This way, she hoped, the donor might start to form a closer relationship with the board member and the Historical Society as a whole. This would come in handy later if they ever needed to make a big ask—that board member would then be in a much better place to arrange the meeting.

Linda put everyone else at tables that didn't have table captains yet.

She also checked in with board members regularly via email to see how they were doing. She asked her board chair to follow up via email as well and make sure people were filling tables.

When the morning of the event came, Linda had most seats accounted for, although it seemed like there was an empty chair at each table. She figured these were just no-shows.

STEP 7: FLESH OUT YOUR PROGRAM

Don't be tempted to be the emcee of the event yourself. You can do in a pinch, but ideally you'll be able to find a volunteer, possibly a board member, to host the event. Look for someone with a proven record of public speaking who is warm, friendly, and can think on their feet.

Put together a detailed schedule of your event and figure out how the time will be divided. Most are an hour, but some run only a half hour. Here's a sample schedule:

7:00 am	Doors open for registration (you'll need at least a couple of volunteers)
7:30 am	Meal is served
7:40 am	Welcome by emcee and introduction of Board Chair
7:45 am	Board Chair welcome and introduction of Executive Director
7:50 am	Executive Director welcome and introduction of first speaker
7:55 am	First speaker presentation
8:10 am	Emcee introduces second speaker
8:12 am	Second speaker presentation
8:25 am	Video screening, introduced by emcee
8:30 am	Emcee talks about what the nonprofit is doing and asks table captains to pass around gift forms
8:40 am	Table captains collect forms, emcee thanks everyone for attending and giving, wrapped up by 8:45.

Adapt this schedule to your own event as needed. It will give you a good sense of how many people you'll need to fill the program and work the event.

STEP 8: MAKE IT A MULTIMEDIA EVENT

If you can find someone willing to donate the time needed to create a video about your organization, take them up on it! Don't sign them up sight-unseen, but look for someone who is willing to help you. At this point, your money should be focused elsewhere.

In addition, you should create a slideshow of pictures of your organization. These should be playing on a loop on a large screen at the beginning and end of the event. Creating a slideshow is easy and free on a computer. Find someone who can help if you're not sure how (this is a great opportunity to engage a volunteer and potential donor). The hard part is getting at least 20 good pictures onto the computer if you don't already have them. Once you've done that, the slideshow is easy.

If you don't have a video, then the slideshow will be more than just background; you'll want people to pay attention and watch it mid-program, so add some inspirational music.

STEP 9: PRINT YOUR COLLATERAL

You're going to need:

• Pledge forms, similar to the reply cards in the mailing above.

• Two copies of a printed list, sorted by last name that shows table assignments. (You should also have a copy sorted by table assignment.)

• Table numbers printed on card stock with card holders of some kind.

• Manila envelopes with pledge forms for each table captain.

• Any brochures you already have describing your organization and its mission.

• Preprinted name tags and blank tags for surprise arrivals.

THE BIG STEP: HOW TO ASK

In some ways, you'll never have an opportunity to ask for money like you will at this event. You can't waste it. You've got to ask big.

Let's look at the groundwork that has been laid from the donor's perspective:

You, the donor, have been invited by a friend to go to a free breakfast, benefiting an organization you like but don't know a lot about. Your friend has let you know a gift would be appropriate, and you've thought ahead and determined a comfortable number. You arrive at breakfast and catch up with your friend before the presentation starts. When it does, you hear the organization's leaders tell you briefly about what they do. Then you listen to a couple of interesting and touching presentations that surprise you and get you interested in a subject that you previously weren't that interested in. Then you're shown a video or a slideshow of the organization doing good work, set to emotionally charged music.

After all that, your friend (not just some random person, but your friend) gives you a pledge form while you listen to how the organization is going to do great things with your money.

You are primed to make a big gift—a big gift for you, that is—larger than the token sum you were prepared to pay when you entered. One of the maxims I believe about fundraising is that it is not about getting donors to "give until it hurts." Donors should "give until it feels good."

Not everyone in the audience is going to react so positively to your message as this ideal donor, and that's fine. They'll give $20 or $50 and be on their way, no matter what amount you ask for. But you can't afford to worry about them; you've got to focus on everyone who got softhearted or weepy-eyed during the presentation. *You can't afford to shoot low.*

The emcee will have a lot of time to make your ask. At least five minutes, maybe more. Have you ever spoken on a topic for five minutes? That's a lot of words! You have a chance now to present a case for giving that is longer and more compelling than any letter could be.

During the ask, the emcee should hit the following points:

- How important the need is, as illustrated before

- How adept the organization is at meeting that need

- How the organization has helped the broader community over many years

- How the organization is looking for your support to continue its good work

- (now would be a good time to have table captains pass out the envelopes)

Then Get to the Ask:

- Ask for a gift of $500. If $500 is low for your organization, ask for $1,000. Or $2,500. Sounds crazy, right? It does, I know. "Consider that a gift of $536 will keep a family of four off the streets for a week" ... "Consider that a gift of $512 means another classroom of students can discover our rich history." ... etc. Some nonprofit breakfasts will already have one or two people at the top levels ready to commit, and will publicly recognize them for that (more on major gifts in the next chapter).

- Ask for $250. Without apologizing for the first ask, tell them what $250 will do.

- Then tell them what $100 will do.

- Then talk about how important their gift is, how important the mission is, how much they are helping the broader community, and so on. Have notes prepared to continue talking about these positive things. The emcee should wrap up when most people are done and move directly to the thank you.

It's not a bad idea to have a photo slideshow going during this as well.

No one is going to feel pressured into giving too much just because you've shot high. No one was at their table telling them they should give $500. True, there is some social pressure at the table, but that's a different thing than a "hard ask." But by aiming high, you've opened the door to even just a few large gifts that you otherwise wouldn't receive. And those gifts will have been given to your organization joyfully by the donor. They will be excited to give you that check. Those few gifts will be profoundly felt on the bottom line when you tally everything up.

By the Numbers ...

Linda filled 22 tables with RSVPs, or 176 people. Of those, only 154 people came. She averaged $100 per gift, many of which were recurring monthly gifts, for a total of $15,400 in revenue.

Her expenses were low: $9/person for food, $600 for printing and postage, $600 for speakers. That's a total of $2,784 in expenses, meaning that she made $12,616 in revenue.

Not only that, but nearly half the people who showed up weren't even in her database. Adding 70 people to your database is a good day ... adding 70 people who just gave an average of $100 is a great day!

All in all, Linda estimated that she'd probably worked just as hard on the breakfast fundraiser as she had on the auction, although this was a lot less stress. Because she'd kept track of her hours while she worked instead of estimating them afterward, she calculated about 150 hours of work between her and her staff. She earned $84/hour ($69/hour after wages paid to the staff), which was less than what she earned with the mailing, but not by much. It was also substantially higher than what she'd gotten out of the auction.

Not only that, but she now had many new names to ask for money in next year's appeal; she'd identified excited donors and volunteers who might make good board members; and she'd successfully gotten a second donation from many donors.

Between the board and staff ask ($1,720), the mailing ($3,940), and the event ($15,400), Linda had raised $21,060 in less a year, a 234% increase over the year before.

She'd done it in only 206 hours and with $3,784 in expenses. If you divide that into $21,060, you can get the ratio of how much it cost her to raise a dollar. For Linda, it cost her 18 cents to raise a dollar. If you factor in staff time, that number goes up to about 33 cents.

As she developed her comfort with the ask, found efficiencies, and identified potential major donors, Linda could certainly find ways to improve. But it was way better than she'd done before.

When Linda presented the totals to the board—all of whom had given a second gift to the Historical Society at the breakfast—she announced the numbers. No one could remember having ever done so well at a single event.

Breakfast Wrap-Up
I like breakfast more than auctions and other fundraising events for

many reasons, but the main reason is simplicity. Get donors inspired and then ask for a big check. There's no work finding and tracking items (one of the most grueling parts of an auction) and no percentage of the donor's money goes to an auction item, so you receive the full amount as a donation.

Start your day with breakfast.

COUNTERPOINT

The one downside of breakfasts is that many non-profits do them. If there are too many, it can feel to donors like they're on a circuit of fundraising breakfasts, paying $50 at each place and moving on.

If you can come up with a better and more creative idea for a fundraiser, by all means go to it. Your donors will thank you for providing something interesting. I've heard about speed-dating fundraisers, fashion show fundraisers, and more.

The key is to try to keep it as simple as possible and as cheap as possible (without being, you know ... cheap.) A fun fundraising idea that gets people interested and excited can bring a lot of new people in the door.

Stick with breakfast for now, but if you have a unique fundraising idea, it's worth scheduling six months later and seeing how it does.

CHAPTER 5

—⚉—

BIG ASKS

THE LAST SKILL we need to address is how to solicit major gifts. If your nonprofit already has some major donors, then the information in this chapter should be part of your fundraising efforts before you send out the solicitation letter in Chapter 3. Major donors should not get mailings asking for money—they should be separated out for more personal asks.

But if you're just venturing in to professional fundraising, you'll need that first year to get a sense of who those major donors are and begin cultivating them for a major ask.

THE DONOR PYRAMID

I mentioned in Chapter 2 the idea of a donor pyramid. The term aptly describes the structure of donors at most nonprofits. At the top of the pyramid are a handful of generous donors; there's a slightly larger group of mid-range donors below them; and the base of the pyramid is made up of many donors who give small gifts. Below that base—the ground, as it were—are the names of the non-donors in your database.

Why is this important?

Because mapping out the donor pyramid is an effective way to identify donors who are likely to "move up" the pyramid.

The pyramid visualization is also important because it shows you where your money comes from. For as many donors as fill in the bottom of the pyramid, most nonprofits get 80% of all giving from just 20% of their donors (and sometimes, 90% of giving from 10% of donors). Looking at your donor pyramid, you should see a similar disparity, where a large amount of what you raised came from the top-most levels of the pyramid.

Let's go back to Linda at the Historical Society. After a year of fundraising, she had a single gift of $500, a small handful of donors who gave between $200 and $300, a larger group who gave around $100, and a much larger group who gave less than $50. The easiest way to raise money from a group like this is to ask the people who gave $200 to $300 to give at the $500 level; to ask the people who gave $100 to give $250; and to ask the people who gave less than $50 to give $100. In other words, to attempt to move as many people as you can up one level on the pyramid.

An organization should be able to get one out of every three to five current donors to go up one level. That means that if Linda had 20 donors who gave $100, she should expect that she could get four or six of them to increase their gift to the next level. The donor pyramid is a very good tool for visualizing this process and identifying the most likely donors to move up.

Once you've established your donor pyramid, your two fundraising goals should be getting new donors into the base of the pyramid and moving current donors up to the next level.

The Donor Pipeline

Of course, increasing a donor from $100 in one year to $250 the next doesn't just magically happen. Donors—especially big ones—need to be primed for an ask. Many fundraising professionals think in terms of a pipeline: a series of steps donors are moved through before making the ask.

The pipeline usually looks something like this:

Identification—For a new donor this would mean getting their contact information. For a current donor this might just mean locating them on the donor pyramid as a target to move up a level.

Cultivation—This is the process of preparing the donor for an ask. Emailed newsletters, invitations to events, and coffee meetings throughout the year are common kinds of cultivation.

Solicitation—The ask. Generally speaking, the higher the amount you ask for, the more cultivation is needed ahead of time and the more personal the ask should be. In the previous sections, I recommended just sending a blanket fundraising appeal to every name you had. For a first-time campaign, it's the way to go. After that, you're going to want to separate out the top 10% or so of donors for a more personal ask, usually phone and face-to-face.

Stewardship—Thanking donors for their gift involves two steps: the thank you to the donor (invitations to special events, a personal note) and the recognition of the gift to the public (such as the annual report).

As is probably obvious, good stewardship blends right back into good cultivation, giving the donor pipeline a circling, or even upwardly spiraling, nature. After that initial step of identification, it's a repeating process of cultivation, solicitation, and stewardship.

The processes described in the first three sections mimic the donor pipeline. Consider the month long process of preparing the board for a gift, the ask over coffee, followed by a thank you with cake at the next board meeting. Consider the structure of the breakfast itself, set up with cultivation (the speeches and video), the ask, and then the thank you. (For the mailing in Section 2, which had no cultivation step before it, I believe that when you have little data or background to go on, you have to start somewhere—and asking is a good place.)

The Eye of the Pyramid

Following the steps in the first three sections gives your nonprofit a good foundation for the pyramid and puts a first trickle of donors into the pipeline. Through those steps, you will have identified a handful of donors who have a strong dedication to your mission and the means to give a large gift. These are the names you want to spend the next year cultivating in preparation for a solicitation.

Strategies for Donor Cultivation

Donor cultivation should not take you away from working on your mission. So far we've been able to keep the amount of fundraising time to a minimum. Let's try to keep it that way.

The first principle to keep in mind is that your donors believe in your mission. Why is that important? Because the best donor cultivation you can do is to include them in your mission. This guiding principle will save you time and energy because—ideally—you won't be spending your time creating unrelated donor events and instead will be connecting your donors even more deeply with you and your mission.

Here are some ways to put this into practice.

DONOR CULTIVATION EVENTS

Remember how I said you should be skeptical of donor cultivation events? Well ... you should be. Especially when you're trying to attract new donors. But when it comes to building relationships with *current* donors, small events become much more practical. Since you're only marketing it to the top 10 to 20% of donors, you don't have as high a cost for invitations, food, and alcohol. And because the attendees are already very likely to give (having given before), the potential reward for spending the time is much greater.

A small community theater might invite its top donors to share some appetizers and wine during intermission or before the show on opening night of a musical. A women's shelter might invite them to attend a lecture by a prominent women's advocate at a local college, followed by a glass of wine at a wine bar. And the Smallville Historical Society might invite donors to go through historic photographs in the archives with a local historian.

Nearly anything related to your mission can be used for a donor cultivation event for top donors. You can tie donors to events already happening—like movies or a musical. You can invite them to an event by a completely different business or nonprofit and attend with them—like a lecture by a speaker on a topic related to your mission. And you can create an event especially for the donors—like going through the photo archives at the Historical Society.

These events should appeal to the donor because they are being offered a special opportunity. It's always good to have a bottle of wine and appetizers to further lure them. But remember: your biggest donors can afford their own food and drink. To get them to come to your donor cultivation event, you need something more than just a little free stuff. Deepening their connection with your mission is the way to do it.

CONNECT THE BOARD

When you have a donor cultivation event—or if you just have a general event donors would be interested in—use the connections already made by the board. Remember that each of your board members called three or more people who gave big during the annual mailing. Remember that if any of those people came to your annual breakfast, you tried to seat them with the board member that called them. You want them to become friends ... or at least friendly. That board member should be the one to invite them to anything. Ideally, the board member should come, too, even if they haven't given as much as the top donors invited. Don't worry about it. It may even help get the board member to increase their own gift next year.

And do keep track of attendance. If one board member regularly gets none of their contacts to attend, then they are probably either not doing the work or are not good at it. Add their donors to another board member's list and see what happens.

CULTIVATION WITHOUT EVENTS

There are other ways to do donor cultivation, and—because they are fast and cheap—email and the Internet are very high on the list.

I strongly recommend against e-newsletters, though. Most people just don't read them, and you want something people will read. Instead, treat those top donors like your friends. Every so often, send a link to an interesting article related to you or your mission with a short note. Assemble the list of email addresses with your board and top donors. Anytime you send anything BE SURE you put the addresses in the BCC (Blind Carbon Copy) line so that you don't accidentally publish email addresses and open people up to too many "Reply All" messages.

An email from a director of a homeless shelter might read:

Hi everyone,

The New York Times had an interesting article today about an incredible woman in Atlanta who's moving mountains and just got 6 new shelters built. Here's the link: [link here]

A very inspirational way to start the day!

Sincerely,

Mary

PS—As usual, let me know if you'd prefer not to get emails like this. No offense will be taken.

Sending out emails like the above invites reflection on the part of the donor, informs them about the world of your nonprofit, and maybe even invites further discussion with donors.

Another option similar to this idea would be blogging, which trades targeted communication for a larger audience. If you are a blogger or have read enough blogs to think you'd be good at it, you could find blogging to be an effective communication tool and a good way to cultivate donors and find new ones. But it doesn't give you the ability to know you are hitting your best donors like a direct email does.

PICK UP THE PHONE!

On the other hand, there are real limits to email and the Internet. When in doubt, pick up the phone. Did you see a donor at the symphony performance last night? Call them and thank them for coming. A phone call has the potential to deepen a relationship much more than an email can.

It's important to note that some donors hate phone calls and prefer emails (or vice versa, or they prefer no communication at all). Use your donor database to flag the donor's preference for communication when you discover a donor's preference (it will usually be pretty clear).

UPGRADE THE DATABASE

Unfortunately, there's no getting around it at this point. You need a real donor database. By this point, if you've downloaded the database template from **www.TheLittleBookOfGold.com** or are using your own Excel spreadsheet or Access database, it's probably getting pretty big. If you're dealing with major gifts, you need to switch.

A donor database will let you target mailings by gift amount, or date of their last gift, or any number of helpful parameters. It will let you flag calls and emails to a donor. You can enter notes about them easily. You can track how many times you've "touched" a donor before an ask. You can sort by gift, by fund, by event, by donor, by pledge, by date ... Yes, you can do many of these things in Excel or Access. But a database *designed* for this is better if you're planning on making asks for $1,000 or more.

I recommend SalsaLabs.com or eTapestry.com as two systems that you can adopt. Each will require some training for you and your staff on using the system, but a well-crafted donor database is an invaluable tool when used well.

MAKING THE ASK

After a year of cultivation since the donor's last gift, you've got to make the ask.

For your top donors, especially those you think you have the best chance of getting a larger gift from, you'll want to make it as personal as possible. Just like with the "high-touch" board asks, the donor needs to know why you've scheduled the face-to-face meeting. You should make the effort to go to them. You should have your "ask" sentence memorized if you're uncomfortable. And you should thank them profusely no matter what their gift is.

For donors who aren't interested in meeting, and thus are much less likely to make a larger gift, you should know that most donors prefer to give in the same manner they did before. So if you aren't successful with the high-touch approach for a donor who gave to your mailing, then send another letter—this time with a personal note from either you or a board member. If they gave at the annual breakfast, make darn sure they get to the breakfast again.

INCREASING GIFTS IS LIKE HITTING IN BASEBALL

If you're a baseball fan, you know that some of the greatest hitters have batting averages in the .300s. This means that for every 1,000 times at bat, they will on average get a hit about a third of a time. Baseball is unusual in that regard: its best players are getting hits only about a third of the time!

With major gift asks, especially when it comes to increasing a current donor's gift, you have to think like a baseball player. If you ask 10 donors to increase their gift from $500 to $1000 and get three to do it, *you did really well*. It sounds good on paper, but that means you'll get turned down for an increase seven times to get those three.

The "numbers" say that if you want to get a major gift—however you define "major"—you need to find three to five people capable of giving that amount and who believe in your mission and your organization.

Find three to five, and you'll get one. (I should note that in the early years of building a fundraising operation from scratch you might find slightly better numbers because you won't yet know the full potential of all your donors.) It's a lot of strikeouts, but if you prepare yourself for it, it won't be so bad.

SETTING UP DONOR LEVELS

You've seen it a million places: Become a "Blue and White supporter"—a "George Washington Donor"—a "Platinum Subscriber." etc. Donor levels like this serve two main purposes:

First, they give the donor something to feel good about in public and in private. One donor might look at your annual report and dream of having enough money to be a platinum donor. But for now, they're a silver donor and they feel good about it. Another donor might want public recognition—such as in the annual report or on a wall plaque—of being in the top circle of donors.

Second, they help define the donor's relationship with your organization. Many donor levels are pitched with certain items, experiences, or services that are benefits of that donor level, tiered with better benefits for higher levels. This helps the donor understand what to expect from you and it also gives you a working job description for managing those donors. If Silver Donors and above get invitations to behind-the-scenes tours, then you'd better make sure you schedule behind-the-scenes tours.

Donor levels have their place, but also come with their own set of traps to watch out for.

The biggest trap: setting them up too early. If your organization is new to professional fundraising as described in the first three sections, you may not know your potential yet. So setting up a Gold Donor Level at $500 is a bad idea if there's a chance that next year your top donors could give $2,000. Now you have to add more levels on top of Gold or redefine it. It gets confusing.

Donor levels should also be set up based on past giving. So if a lot of donors give $300, $400 might be a good cutoff for a donor level because it encourages some of those people to increase their gift. But if you don't have past data, you can't make these calls. My recommendation is to wait at least a year, maybe two, to see how giving looks before setting up donor levels.

The next trap is overly complex levels. Some nonprofits, especially in the arts, have certain benefits frequently associated with donor levels. If you need to know the benefits associated with 10 different levels, both you and your donors will be confused and you're liable to forget something and upset a donor.

And finally, don't include everyone. For starting off a donor level, I believe the best course is targeting the top two-thirds of your donor pyramid. For example, you might set donor levels at $250, $500, and $1000, and not include any lower levels. There are a few reasons for this: it keeps your focus at the top where the money is; it keeps things from getting too complex; and it means you don't have to give any "benefits" to any donor who isn't paying substantially for it.

It's a Donation, Don't Make It a Purchase

When you start to think of whether you want to add benefits to donor levels, think long and hard before adding a benefit. *Anything* you put in the box of "Gold Donor" (or whatever your level is) you're going to have to do.

Did you promise them a *Time Out Film Guide* (as we promised our top donors at the Grand Cinema one year)? All right. Now you have to buy the guide and figure out how to get the two-pound book to your donors. If they don't pick it up it's going to sit on your desk gathering dust and reminding you that you're either going to have to drive it out to them or mail it, another expense you might not have counted on. And even though the donor hasn't come to pick it up as she promised she would, sometime during the year she's going to remember it and wonder why you haven't followed through on your promise.

It might have seemed like a good idea to give a $15 book to get a $500 gift. But I learned it was also a headache. What seemed so simple was not so simple for a small nonprofit like ours.

Consider, too, a community theater that offers a "Star Subscriber" donor level at $300. For that, the donor gets two free tickets to every show (estimated value: $200), and two free tickets to the auction (estimated value: $80), and a quarterly newsletter. It might seem like the donor is shelling out a lot of cash, but the actual *gift* they're giving is about $20 plus whatever portion of the auction tickets are a donation. (I'll follow up on this common occurrence more in the next chapter).

And finally, consider a nonprofit with a top donation level of $5,000, which includes a special party for its top donors. If you have only one top donor ... how much of a party is that going to be, and how much is it going to cost you to throw it for just them?

The key to good donor levels is to keep the list of benefits light. I'll reiterate: it's a donation, not a purchase. Special experiences—like the donor cultivation events described above—make for good "added value" benefits. Be wary of adding too many services. Most donors to small nonprofits don't need a lot in return—except your sincere thanks and continued good work.

COUNTERPOINT

Sometimes it's possible to bypass the donor pipeline, or at the very least, speed it up. Let's say a wealthy donor gives you $2,500. It is very likely this person has friends who could make a similar gift.

Find opportunities to bring this person further in to your circle. Could he host a table at a fundraiser? Could he host a private 'salon' event at his home for his friends with a special speaker? Could he join your board? Getting him to help you fundraise will open new doors for you.

The initial gifts from his friends could be much larger because his presence vouches for you.

This is not a relationship that should be thought of as being crass. Be honest and sincere. Connect over your shared vision for your organization or for the mission. If you want him to do something, like host a salon, ask for it using the same technique you asked for a gift earlier. If he can't, that's all right.

By leveraging the relationships of others around you, your fundraising growth can be incredibly strong. Just make sure you are approaching it in a professional and respectful manner.

PART I SUMMARY

—∞—

THE DEVELOPMENT PLAN

THE FIRST PART of this book forms the backbone of a process for asking for individual donations ...

- We started with highly effective, "high-touch" asks to those closest to the nonprofit: the board and staff.

- We then asked those closest to the nonprofit with a professional solicitation letter and a strong thank you and follow-up.

- Then, in order to increase the size of our starting pool of donors, we held a fundraising event that brought in new donors and made a substantial sum of money.

- During that time we identified the most likely major donors and prepared them for a larger ask.

That's your development plan right there. If you took those strategies and hung numbers on them—number of donors, average gift size—you would get a really good sense of your potential for the year.

After the first year, you'll be able to get a good forecast for the next year, too, because you're not doing anything new, just increasing the number of contacts. You're moving big donors up the pyramid and bringing in new donors at the bottom. This is a "virtuous cycle," where successes of one year make the successes of the next year more attainable. It's sustainable, it's professional, and it's repeatable, year after year.

PART TWO

BUILDING CAPACITY

CHAPTER 6

—∭—

FINDING NEW DONORS

THERE ARE STILL some opportunities nonprofits have that bring in new donors with a minimum of work. Don't fall into the temptation to continue creating new schemes—new events, new ways to ask—instead of shepherding basic fundraising programs. Creating new schemes takes time and energy! And implementing them takes even more.

Your goal should not be to create more fundraising events or new and improved ways to ask for money. The goal now is to plug as many names into the cycle you've created as possible.

There are two main ways to do this:
1) Collect, as passively as possible, small donations.
2) Collect names, addresses, and email addresses to add to your database.

DONORS SHOULD FIND THEMSELVES

That's not meant to be a spiritual statement. But for the most successful fundraising program, donors should "self-identify," meaning that they give you their contact information directly before they give.

Be wary about soliciting for donations from a list provided by another nonprofit. You may collect some money from it, but for many people on the list it will feel like they've been asked out of the blue. Don't waste your resources.

(An important note: lists from other organizations can be helpful to *marketing*. A symphony that wants to find new subscribers has every reason to send marketing material to a list from a local opera company. But they should not send a request for donations. I'll cover this important distinction in a moment.)

Your goal, therefore, should be to have as many opportunities for donors to self-identify as possible.

ECONOMIES OF SCALE

Intuitively, it's easy to understand that more names in the database equals more money (assuming that the names are from people who have self-identified). But there is another big benefit to increasing your database. Not only are you making more money, you're doing it more efficiently.

Consider that the amount of time it takes to solicit 3,000 people via a mailing is not much different than the time it takes to solicit 1,000 people. At the very least, it's not three times more work. In other words, as your database grows, you become more efficient. So adding names raises your "hourly rate."

GET THOSE NAMES!

If you have any place where potential donors might come through—such as the lobby of the performance hall you're renting, a booth at the farmers market, a storefront office, or a pioneer cabin—you should always have a clipboard for collecting names and addresses. A simple form for this can be found online.

Whenever possible, have a volunteer stationed with the clipboard and form. In my experience, email addresses are easier to ask for than full mailing addresses because it takes less work for the donor to sign up. The downloadable template form has spaces for everything with name and email first. If the donor wants to fill out more, great!

While email addresses are easier for quick collection, mailing addresses are still more valuable for solicitations. Aim for mailing addresses when you have more of a "one-on-one" opportunity, and not when you're grabbing the attention of people on the go.

THE ONLINE ASK

The two goals of this chapter are passively collecting small donations and getting names added to the database. Having a prominent ask on your website fulfills both those goals.

This can be as easy as creating PayPal and Google Checkout accounts for your organization and then cutting and pasting code for each to your site. If you're not sure how to tackle this, get help from a friend. It requires just a little knowledge of HTML, but once it's up and working, any visitor to your website now has the opportunity to give.

Don't expect a lot of people to take advantage of this, however. The number of donors who will give to you randomly over the Web is a very low percentage of your total site traffic—usually less than 1%. But for just a little bit of up front work, you can grab stray $10 and $20 donations. Someone willing to donate money to you on a whim is a good person to have in your database for future asks.

Also, you can start including the option in your annual solicitation. For people for whom you only have email addresses, including a link to a donations page is a good way to potentially increase giving—especially from younger donors more comfortable paying over the Internet.

COLLECT LOOSE CHANGE

This doesn't get you names, but passively collecting loose change has the power to add up, if you can collect enough of it. Just look at the bell ringers outside of grocery stores every Christmas: they get a small amount of change from a small percentage of people who walk by them. But with a large enough crowd, even that adds up. If you run any kind of retail operation, you should put out a jar with a note about donations. (Be clear it's not a tip for the person behind the counter.)

When I ran the Grand Cinema, we put out a jar on the concessions counter and collected on average 4 cents from every person that came to see a movie. It doesn't sound like much, but we sold 100,000 tickets annually, meaning that we got $4,000 from that small jar every year.

To reduce the likelihood of theft, we chose an old heavy milk bottle—easy to get money in and hard to get money out. We also secured the bottle to the counter with lots of Velcro.

This kind of thing doesn't get you names or addresses, but if you have access to a high volume of people, you can make strong gains here.

KNOW WHEN YOU'RE SELLING AND WHEN YOU'RE ASKING

I really want to highlight this distinction. It applies most specifically to organizations whose customer base is also their most likely donor base (like arts and civic organizations), but there are lessons here for all nonprofits.

Consider Linda at the Historical Society. They had been asking for a suggested donation of $5 per person at the Pioneer Cabin. But they were collecting, on average, only $1.50 per person. Linda decided that this practice needed to stop. She, the board, and the volunteers and staff person that worked in the cabin didn't treat the suggested donation as a "strongly" suggested donation, where it's difficult to get in without paying the suggested amount (as many nonprofits with this structure do). This is one of those times when what works for a national museum may not work for small nonprofits.

Having a passive ask—a small sign asking for a donation—was clearly not effective for the Historical Society. Linda decided to implement a ticket price for the cabin.

Because she had the data from the previous year, she had enough information to set a fair market price for the tour. Linda decided to charge $3/ticket. At the same time, she created a monthly "free day" at the Pioneer Cabin every third Thursday that corresponded with a free day to another local museum. (Important note: Linda most certainly got this approved by Board of Directors before she implemented this strategy.)

By charging a flat ticket price twice the amount of the average donation she's previously received Linda expected that she would nearly double annual revenue generated from the cabin. Linda was assuming that the change to $3/person likely wasn't expensive enough to stop people from coming. This assumption was likely true for the Historical Society, but it may not be true for all organizations. Good data and common sense will usually be enough to decide what would work for your nonprofit.

Yes, from the few families who previously gave $20 for a family of four, she would now get only $12. But she still was going to make more in the long run. In addition, she'd separated entry to the Pioneer Cabin from donated support. Psychologically, this was a very good decision for the nonprofit because it separated "attending" from "supporting." It emphasized that there is a value to touring the cabin, separating it from support of the Historical Society.

Separating attendance from support requires a mental—even philosophical—change in thinking about your organization and how you communicate with the public. This is a distinction I want to make clear, so I'll give another example.

Consider a nonprofit community theater that wants to increase attendance. Far too often, it asks people to "support" the theater and come see a musical. Doesn't this subconsciously tell people that paying to see a musical is an act of charity in and of itself? In fact, doesn't it even tell people that the musical isn't actually worth the ticket price? I know that sounds a little harsh, but consider how odd it would be if a restaurant asked for your "support" instead of asking you to come and enjoy a meal.

I hear you saying, "But that's a completely different thing! A restaurant is a business, not a nonprofit." Of course it is. But think of the patron who has $20 left to spend on entertainment this month. She can spend that money on something fun, by going to see a baseball game or going to a restaurant, or she can "support" an organization, by going to see a musical. People don't want to "support" anything with their entertainment dollar. They want to have fun, or be inspired, or maybe even learn something new, depending on what interests them. Could they do those things at your nonprofit? Most likely. But by asking for their "support," you are signaling that for them to come is an act of altruism—that your activity is *not fun*. Instead of being asked to *buy* an experience (the musical), our hypothetical and potential patron is being asked to *give* her money (as support).

This isn't a semantic argument. It's an argument about how to value your nonprofit's services. The default mode of nonprofits seems to be always asking. But we need to know when it's better to sell.

If I still haven't convinced you, then consider this final question. Let's say the community theater has successfully persuaded someone to "support" it by attending the musical. How much less likely is that person to "support" the theater when it really needs it—with an annual appeal? Isn't their response going to be, "But I just supported them by seeing that musical!" and tossing the ask aside?

NEXT STEP: ANNUAL MEMBERSHIPS AND SUBSCRIPTIONS

If you have a set ticket price, annual memberships and subscriptions become appealing fundraising tools. My advice still stands: this is not about asking for "support." Generally speaking, these programs should be designed to "save money" for regular customers, and should be marketed that way, not as a way to support the nonprofit.

I put "save money" in quotation marks because most people overestimate how often they use subscriptions and memberships. At the Grand Cinema, a survey told us that people estimated they came to the theater 10 times a year when in fact ticket collection data showed us it was half that. The membership rate was a great deal for those who really did come 10 times a year, but for those who came less it wasn't much different than just paying for tickets at the door (but gave us a steadier income).

We took that concept further and started offering a free small popcorn to any member. The cost to us was negligible; most people wanted more than just a small so they didn't take advantage of it; and those who did would frequently buy a drink to go with their popcorn. And thanks to offering the small popcorn, we sold *many* more memberships. A small free item brought in thousands of dollars in memberships.

I recommend an annual membership drive, aimed at getting previous members to sign up again and persuading current customers to join. A special promotion is usually the way to go, as long as the benefit you offer is not expensive—an extra guest pass, free popcorn, and the like. Try to avoid paying $5 for a tangible good to get a $40 membership. Not only can you do better, but you'll probably end up with leftover items, giving you an extra cost that further eats in to your margin.

There are exceptions in which a membership might be better billed as "support" than as a way to save money. Linda at the Historical Society decided that no one came to the pioneer cabin often enough that it made sense to bill an annual membership as a way to save money. She wanted to charge at least $40 for a membership (it would increase her average donation), but at $3/ticket to the Pioneer Cabin, it was unlikely it would be "a deal" for anyone. Instead, she billed the membership program as a way to support the Historical Society and offered free attendance for a year as a "thank you."

It can go either way, but the key is to make sure you know what works best for your nonprofit. Know when you're selling and know when you're asking.

CHAPTER 7

—∿∿—

GRANT REQUESTS

I LOVE GRANTS. Everyone should love grants. The foundation lays everything out for you: this is what they do fund, this is what they don't, this is when you should ask, this is the form you should fill out, and this is the information they need. Imagine if all individual donors made things as clear as that!

Some nonprofits are funded almost exclusively by grants. If you're one of those, I hope the first sections of this book can open up a new revenue stream of individual donations. In fact, it's incredibly important that you do so. Grants have a way of falling off over time, and if there's a single grant that represents a quarter or more of your income, you'll want to do everything to decrease your reliance on that grant.

Alternatively, if you're just putting a toe into the grant waters for the first time, I hope this will give you a good start.

WHERE TO FIND GRANTS

There are online resources for finding grants—the most recognizable is at Guidestar.org, which charges a monthly or annual subscription for the service. There are also books with grant lists in them published regularly, although they are usually even more expensive.

But the best place to start is with peer nonprofits. Look locally and then move to regional, state, and even national levels. Find a copy of their annual report (often online) and look for their foundations and agency donors. If you research those foundations, you'll get a good sense of whether you might also qualify.

Is it unethical to do this kind of digging? No, it's smart! You are researching foundations by searching for the nonprofits they currently fund. If you fit their qualifications, then there is no reason you shouldn't apply, and it doesn't matter where you heard about them.

BE YOURSELF

The first thing you need to know is that no one's going to give you money if you're not honestly portraying what your organization does. Don't stretch what you do to try to fit into the box of a granting organization. If you're not a good fit, don't spend the time.

A foundation that gives money for "basic needs" likely won't give to the Historical Society. A foundation that gives to "community enrichment," however, might be a good fit.

During the application process, it's important to "be yourself" as well. Don't pretend to be larger than you are, or smaller than you are, or more diverse, or whatever it is you might be worried about. Think about the grant application as you would a job application: you need to be prepared to back up whatever goes on the application form.

RESEARCH, THEN PICK UP THE PHONE

If you've never applied to a foundation, it's worth calling ahead and finding out more about them. But before you do, make sure you get as many of your questions answered on the foundation's website as possible. You don't want to waste the grant manager's time with easy questions you could have gotten answered online.

Once you're ready to call, you'll want to find out as much as you can about what the foundation looks for. Remember, grant managers for foundations are very much like donors. They might not actually have control of the purse strings themselves, but don't think they are out of the process. Treat them as you would your best donor.

Here are some good questions you want to know the answers to either from the website, or the grant manager:

• *Do you regularly give to organizations like [fill in the blank]?* If a foundation doesn't routinely fund food banks, and you're a food bank, you're going to want to know that. (This is especially important if you are a religiously based nonprofit, which can often be excluded from grant programs.) If you ask this question, the grant manager will make it clear whether they think your organization is a good fit. Usually, it's worth listening to their advice.

• *Do you fund operational expenses?* (Another way to put it might be

"Do you give unrestricted gifts?") Some foundations give to specific programs or items, others will simply give to the organization that has gone through their screening process and will let the organization put the money where they most need it. What they give will affect what you ask for.

- *How big is your average gift?* For your first application, you probably shouldn't ask for an amount above the average gift size.

- *What strengths do you look for during the review process?* This starts to get a little nebulous, but it's still worth trying to get a handle on. You might hear answers like "community-building," "financial stability," "creativity and innovation," "organizational capacity," or any number of buzzwords. Here you're looking for the frame for your own application. If the foundation likes to see "organizational capacity," you'll need to speak to your trustworthiness, your track record managing projects, and your success stories. If they like "community-building," then you'll need to speak to your role bringing people together toward a common goal, working with the public, and partnering with other nonprofits. You still have to be yourself, as I said before, but this gives you a frame to describe what you do.

- *Can you tell me a little bit about reporting?* It's worth finding out in advance what you'll have to do if you get the money. It also lets them know you think ahead.

CALL YOUR BOARD CHAIR

I know, I know, that's always my advice. But before you send out a grant application, it's a good idea to give a "heads up" to your board chair. First, it's good to let them know you're hard at work. Second, they might have some experience—positive or negative—with the foundation you're interested in. And third, some granting agencies and foundations ask for a board chair's signature on the application or ask for an interview with you and your board chair. So you're giving advance notice of what will be expected.

BE THOROUGH AND DON'T CHEAT

When you apply for a grant application, make sure you answer every question and include everything asked for. Know that many foundations ask for the same thing in an application. So if you need a copy of the 501c3 certification from the IRS, make 10 copies for future applications and file them appropriately.

You also *must* have a proofreader. There's no reason to let grammatical mistakes hurt your chances.

As to the "don't cheat" rule ... I hope it's obvious why cheating is bad. But let me put it another way: a good grant reviewer can often tell when things don't add up.

BE SPECIFIC

It's a hallmark of good writing that the specific is better than the general, and it often applies to grants as well. Be specific with what you'd like to do with the money. For your first grant from an organization, the more specific you can be, the better. Even if the organization gives to "operational expenses," I would still recommend that you be specific on the first ask, and save those more general asks for when your nonprofit's relationship to the foundation is stronger.

PLAN FOR PROCRASTINATION

If you tend to put things off, just know that grant applications take a long time, so plan ahead. Don't schedule anything for the day a grant application is due and expect to spend the full day getting everything together, especially if you're new to the process. Reread the application materials carefully. I speak from experience: you don't want to find out an hour before the application is due that you actually need five copies of everything.

ONE YEAR LATER: CAN YOU ASK FOR MORE?

If you have successfully received a grant from a foundation, a common practice is to increase the amount you ask for the next year. My recommendation is to do it if you can truly justify it—that is, if you have a program or a purchase or something that really fits with what the foundation likes to fund.

You can also ask your contact at the foundation for their advice.

CHAPTER 8

—◠◠—

REALLY BIG ASKS: PLANNED GIVING
AND CAPITAL CAMPAIGNS

E VEN THOUGH THIS is a book for "small and very small nonprofits" you should know some basics about the world of really big asks: mainly planned giving and capital campaigns. If something falls out of the sky or if you are suddenly forced into needing a major campaign, this section gives you a base of knowledge from which to work. Let's start with planned giving.

PLANNED GIVING AND ENDOWMENTS

"Planned giving" is a broad term that describes numerous kinds of gifts a donor can give to a nonprofit. But often, when people say "planned giving," what they mean are gifts to your nonprofit in their estate.

These kinds of gifts can be huge windfalls for any nonprofit. They represent an opportunity for giving unequaled during a person's lifetime. After all, it might be hard to give 40% of your assets to a nonprofit while you're alive, but it's a lot easier when you're not.

Because of the difficult subject matter of planned giving, though, most nonprofits don't address it with donors because they are simply afraid to bring it up. Creating a strategy for planned giving will give you an opportunity many nonprofits aren't taking advantage of.

THE WONDERS OF COMMUNITY FOUNDATIONS

I believe a good first step is making contact with your local community foundation. If you're not sure that your community has one, check out **www.cof.org/Locator** for a state-by-state search.

Community foundations are highly regional foundations that serve two main functions. They manage large funds for donors and they manage endowments for nonprofits. They usually support themselves by taking a percentage of the money they manage. The benefit to donors is that they have an organization handling all donation requests, an organization that uses its knowledge of the local conditions to select the most worthy applicants. And the benefit to nonprofits is not having to manage and invest their own endowment.

Community foundations also have far more experience than most other nonprofits when it comes to planned giving. If you find a donor who is interested in planned giving, a community foundation can link you and that donor with a certified financial planner (CFP) who specializes in this kind of thing.

And you need a CFP! Don't try to help someone with their will in-house. It's a bad idea. You need a professional, and a community foundation is a good place to start for that resource.

An Endowment?

For most small nonprofits, creating an endowment from your own reserve funds is usually just not worth it. Since you can't expect any more than 5% of the principle from an endowment, putting $100,000 into one would net you only $5,000/year. Most small nonprofits would rather have that capital more readily available in a money market or a CD.

But if a donor wants to give a portion of their estate through planned giving, that's a great way to start or build on an endowment. Since you weren't expecting the money it's much easier to lock it away in an endowment. It also recognizes that the major gift from the donor will last forever. A donation of $100,000 into an endowment will pay many more times the original amount over the years.

Again, I would recommend that the endowment be managed by your local community foundation to take the onus of management off your shoulders.

Planting the Seed

If you're new to it, planned giving should be done fairly passively. Put a small advertisement for it in a newsletter or annual report. Something like, "What kind of legacy will you leave? If you have considered leaving a legacy for the Historical Society, please call ... " could work well.

Publicly thank a donor for their planned gift (assuming the donor is all right with that) and use it as an opportunity to describe the benefits of planned giving to both the donor and to your nonprofit (your community foundation or local nonprofit center will have more information if you need it). Just keep putting the message in front of donors as often and as passively as you can.

And the easiest method might just be to put a check box on the reply card of your annual giving solicitation next to the words, "I would like more information about planned giving."

INVITE DONORS TO A FINANCIAL PLANNING SEMINAR

This has nothing to do with the mission of your nonprofit. But if you have a significant number of donors who are past or near retirement age, getting them to a financial planning seminar is a good idea.

Many large nonprofits in your area already likely host an event for donors at which they talk about financial planning, with a portion dealing with estate planning. You just may not know about them because, well, you're probably not in the target audience.

If your local community foundation doesn't host an event like this, check with the development department of any large museums, hospitals, or colleges in your area. See if you can arrange for your donors to attend.

DON'T BUDGET FOR PLANNED GIVING

The truth is, it's almost impossible to figure out what you might get from planned giving. That's why I like the solution of putting all planned gifts into an endowment, unless a donor specifically says otherwise. You can budget for what comes out of an endowment and it will provide stable, long-term income. Endowments are wonderful things for a nonprofit, and planned gifts are a great way to build them.

"WHEN WE HAVE A CAPITAL CAMPAIGN ..."

Most board members and most nonprofit managers have never been through a successful capital campaign before. And yet, everyone has seen another nonprofit do it, and so many believe they can do it, too. The truth is, capital campaigns are massive undertakings that will dwarf any project your nonprofit has accomplished to date. So look with great skepticism on any statement that begins, "When we have a capital campaign ..."

I want you to know one important thing about a capital campaign ... you probably can't do it. I hope that's not too harsh, but I want to save you some trouble.

Small (and especially very small) nonprofits usually are in no way equipped to embark on a capital campaign. If you don't believe me, I'll take you through the math below and you'll get a sense of why it is so daunting.

How Much Do You Need to Raise?

For argument's sake, let's say your nonprofit has an opportunity worth considering: maybe a piece of available land for a new women's shelter. You've assembled a team of professionals who estimate that between land and building costs, it will cost you $2.5 million for the project (counting all soft costs like taxes and the architect's fees). So now you know what you need to raise, right?

Sorry. You're not there yet. Let's do a little back of the envelope math ...

First, have you considered how long it's going to take you to raise $2.5 million? Done well, most capital campaigns will take about two to three years. What will land and building prices be like then? It's a good bet they'll all be more expensive. For this exercise, let's just figure costs will go up 3% every year, which means you'll need to raise about $2.75 million.

Second, you'll want to spend a lot of time figuring out if your new building is going to result in any higher annual operating costs. It would be a really bad idea to raise $2.75 million and then find out you don't have the capacity to run the building once you've opened it (unfortunately, this happens to nonprofits way too often). Having done the budgeting, you realize your new building will cost you another $50,000/year to operate in utilities, maintenance, and staff. So we'll add three years of additional operating costs to the total, as part of a transition fund. Now we're at $2.9 million, *a full $400,000 more than where we started.*

Third—and I know you're going to hate this one—you need to pay for your fundraising costs. Think back to the earlier sections; we regularly calculated how much it takes to raise a dollar. Just like that, capital campaigns have costs as well. They aren't free. Let's say that your organization can raise money for 25 cents on the dollar. So let's figure that since capital campaigns are generally more efficient than regular fundraising, you can do it for 20 cents on the dollar. That still means it will cost you $580,000 to raise $2.9 million. Where is that money going to come from? Unfortunately, it's going to have to come from the campaign itself. So our new goal is $3.48 million, which we'll round up to $3.5 million.

See how quickly a building that was going to cost $2.5 million went up 40% in price—a full million dollars you didn't count on?

Now ... Can You Raise It?

Before starting this section, I have to emphasize that this is for rudimentary budgeting and estimating *only*. A quick snapshot, if you will. And my goal is still to convince you that you probably can't make your target.

So let's just stick with our goal of $3.5 million. This part gets hard. Even if you have increased giving by 400% in just a couple years, you still might not be ready to tackle a huge project like a capital campaign.

To raise $3.5 million, you have to play by the "80/20" rule. That rule says that 80% of the money you need will come from just 20% of capital campaign donors. (This is pretty much the same for annual giving too, and like that, your real numbers might be more like 90/10.)

Your math should be based off of your current donor base, because it's not a good idea to budget for gifts from anyone who is not currently a donor. That means that—most likely—you'll be looking to the top 20% of your donors for about $2.8 million and the bottom 80% for the remaining $700,000.

How can you tell if your donors even have the ability to give you that kind of money? We're going to take two key points to figure this out.

- Point 1—The capacity of a donor for a capital campaign is between 10 and 25 times their annual gift.

- Point 2—As described before, to get one major gift you need to ask three to five people capable at giving at that level.

Regarding Point 1, start by considering your own giving. If you give a $100 annually to a nonprofit, you are *probably* capable of giving between $1,000 and $2,500 to it over a period of three years. (Most capital campaign gifts are given over a period of time, maybe even as much as five years.) Capital campaign gifts, especially the biggest ones, are usually not given from a donor's income, either; they are given from the donor's asset base, which enables larger gift amounts.

These are both estimates, but they'll get you in the ballpark as you figure out whether you can get close to your capital campaign goal. With these two points, the math becomes pretty easy:

- Add up what the top 20% of donors give to your nonprofit.

- Multiple it by 25 to account for donor capacity (see Point 1).

- Divide it by 3 to account for only a percentage of donors giving (see Point 2).

- Compare it to 80% of what you need to raise.

- Repeat for the bottom 80% donors and compare it to the remaining 20% of what you need to raise.

Know that this will give you a highly optimistic number.
Here's what that formula would look like with the numbers filled in:

- The top 20% of donors to my nonprofit give $80,000 annually.

- $80,000 multiplied by 25 = $2 million.

- $2 million divided by 3 = $666,666.

- Compare that to whatever we need to raise.

Repeating it for the bottom 80%, we get this:

- The bottom 80% of donors give $50,000 annually.

- $50,000 multiplied by 25 = $1.25 million.

- $1.25 million divided by 3 = $416,666.

- Compare that to whatever we need to raise.

So in total, my organization, with annual giving of $130,000, could probably raise about $1.1 million ($666,666 plus $416,666). If we were the nonprofit that wanted to raise $3.5 million for a building, we would have a very hard time getting there.

You Need Professional Help

Again, the above exercise is for planning and rudimentary budgetary purposes only. It's a way to figure out quickly whether you could get close to your goal, or to get a sense of what a realistic goal might be.

For anything beyond this level of estimating, and I *strongly* recommend you find a consulting firm to work with you. Consulting firms regularly work with nonprofits to assess the viability of capital campaigns. They have strong analytical tools, they survey key donors, and they can come up with a good estimate of how much a particular project might be able to raise.

And capital campaigns really are about the individual project. The same set of donors might be able to raise $3.5 million for a new shelter but only $2 million for a new headquarters. Certain projects will strike a fire and certain projects won't.

For Further Information

Let's say that you have a project that fits within what you think you can raise, or let's say that you have no other choice and you have to move forward anyway (it goes without saying this is a bad place to try to raise money from). A professional consulting firm will help you through this process, but if you are interested, I've broken out a typical 36-month capital campaign schedule online.

If your nonprofit has been talking about having a capital campaign "someday," do the math and decide for yourself how likely it is. The worst thing in the world is to see a nonprofit banking on a campaign that has no hope of success.

Counterpoint

Depending on your situation, there might be good reason to go out and ask for planned gifts. If you've been through a year of fundraising and feel like your relationships with donors are strong; if you feel like you have a compelling reason for them to give; if you feel you have the professional assistance to make it work … it's worth exploring more than just the "passive" ask recommended before.

Keep in mind that the larger the gift, the more cultivation and the more planning go in to it. But if you have the relationships, the reason, and the expertise, a successful planned giving campaign could secure the future of your nonprofit for years to come.

FINAL THOUGHTS

—∿—

How to Stay Small No Matter How Big You Get

THERE ARE REAL strengths to being a small nonprofit. You are quick to react; you have low overhead; and there are no huge hierarchies separating the executive director from the "ground floor" of the operation.

I believe that if you grow using the processes described in this book, you can still maintain those strengths while you become more financially stable and secure and do even more good with the money you raise.

Should You Hire Development Staff?

I started this book by encouraging you to put off hiring a development director and to do the fundraising yourself. I hope that by this point you've seen how doable some of these tasks are.

That doesn't mean you should never hire development staff. Before you think about hiring for this position, it's good to know what they do. Most development directors are responsible for managing daily fundraising operations like mailings, phone-a-thon calling nights, and fundraising events. They are responsible for managing donor stewardship, for identifying prospective donors, and for making some level of personal asks.

Having a development director does not remove all fundraising responsibilities from the executive director. Executive directors should expect to still do regular donor cultivation and solicitation in concert with development staff.

So, with that said, let's talk about when to hire.

My first recommendation would be that if you are ready to hire development staff, don't hire a development "director." Hire a part-time development "coordinator," or a part-time and seasonal "event planner" for your annual breakfast specifically. Or even just hire a part time clerical worker to help you with data entry, gift processing, stewardship, and some of the other minutiae of development (plus whatever else you might have around the office). A development "director" will likely cost you too much. Do most large nonprofits have development directors with a large development staff? Yes. But that doesn't mean you need to jump right in.

As a loose rule of thumb, I'd hire someone for only as much work as you're putting into fundraising. If your "billable hours" show you're putting in 15 hours a week into fundraising, hire someone for 15 hours a week. You'll probably still spend eight hours a week managing them and making asks, but your capacity to raise money has increased and your actual cost to raise money has dropped slightly (since you're paying the part time person less than what you make).

Don't Be Afraid of Security

If I were offered the chance to run any nonprofit in the world, I would choose a small nonprofit ... a small nonprofit sitting on a big pile of money, that is.

Many nonprofits are scared to amass cash. They feel that a donor gave them $1,000, so why should it sit in the bank? Every year they end up breaking even or maybe end slightly in the red.

First I should clarify that if a donor has given you $1,000 for a particular program or with any other restrictions, you are obligated to follow the donor's wishes. But not every donor will give a restricted gift. In addition, if you are receiving earned revenue it's absolutely all right to say "this $1,000 from a donor will pay for X program, while this $1,000 in revenue is going into the bank." It has the same net effect as if you put $1,000 from a donor into the bank, but it is still different. (I recommend talking with your bookkeeper about ways to track where money is coming from in your books. It is a great thing to be able to show donors exactly how their gift was used.)

You don't have to spend every dollar you bring in. If you don't already have a three month contingency fund—money that could sustain your nonprofit for three months if no revenue came in—then that should be an early goal.

For some nonprofits, a three-month contingency fund might mean banking more than $100,000. Good. A nonprofit with a healthy bank account is more likely to get grant requests and won't need to raise money from a position of fear and desperation. Like all rules, of course, this one could be taken out of context. A nonprofit with *10 times* its annual budget or more saved up is far less likely to get grants or donors. But having reserves of three to even 12 months of operating expenses is in your favor. After that, you'll probably want to start either buying non-cash assets or creating an endowment.

SAY YES MORE

At the Grand Cinema, I worked very hard to say "yes" whenever I could. When an amateur filmmaker would come in and ask to screen a movie for their family and friends, we would accommodate them as well as possible by opening early on a Saturday or moving around showtimes on a Monday evening. It meant inconveniences to the staff sometimes. But to that one filmmaker and their 30 friends and family, the Grand was *beloved* for what we did. If you want to be a part of your community, listen to what your community wants and bend over backwards to provide it.

It's "bottom up" planning because it will open up potential that you previously wouldn't have thought of. If the Grand hadn't opened itself to filmmakers in that way, we wouldn't have been able to see the need to serve filmmakers. We wouldn't have created an entirely new portion of the Grand's revenue—providing services to filmmakers through competitions, festivals, and workshops—that helped stabilize the theater and allow us to serve our mission better than we ever had.

You can find new revenue possibilities and become a better part of your community all at the same time. Just say yes more.

RESOURCES
—m—

FURTHER DEVELOPMENT READING

- *Donor-Centered Fundraising* by **Penelope Burke.** A standard for any nonprofit looking to continue building its fundraising.

- *The Non-Profit Handbook* by **Gary M. Grobman.** A handy reference guide for nonprofit managers.

- *The Seven Faces of Philanthropy* by **Russ Alan Prince.** and Karne Maru File A guide for approaching major donors.

FURTHER BUSINESS/ADMINISTRATION READING

- *The E-Myth Revisited* by **Michael E. Gerber.** This book is tailored to entrepreneurs and small businesses. But there is great knowledge in here on management in general, especially management of a small team, customer relations, and administrative structuring. It's very readable, too.

- *Getting Things Done* by **David Allen.** I can't recommend this book on personal productivity highly enough. I never would have completed writing this book if I hadn't adopted the "GTD" system recommended by David Allen.

- *Mission-Based Management* by **Peter C. Brinckerhoff.** This book provides a strong overview of running a nonprofit to a new manager. I found a lot of strength here and turned to it often while working at various nonprofits.

- *Who Moved My Cheese?* by **Spencer Johnson.** In addition to being a "self-help" book, this book may also help you if your nonprofit is having difficult times.

ONLINE DOCUMENTS

Here is a list of all the online documents referenced in the text. They can all be downloaded from **www.thelittlebookofgold.com/index. php/downloads**.

- **Donor Database:** A spreadsheet to accommodate an initial donor database. Recommended for nonprofits just starting their fundraising efforts. Eventually, you should choose an online donor database system. *(Excel)*

- **Fundraiser Budget:** A budget worksheet for a breakfast fundraiser. *(Excel)*

- **Reply Card:** A sample reply card. *(Word)*

- **Sign-Up Sheet:** For collecting addresses. *(Word)*

- **Solicitation Letter:** A sample ask letter for the Smallville Historical Society. *(Word)*

- **Table Captain Guide:** Tips for table captains. *(Word)*

ONLINE FORUMS

Talk to other nonprofit leaders at **www.fundraisinghat.com**. It's specifically built for those who run small nonprofits and want to share ideas and ask questions of each other about fundraising.

GLOSSARY

Advancement: Just as fundraising became "development," so too has "development" become "advancement" in some circles. It can be considered synonymous with development and fundraising.

Annual Fund / Annual Giving / Annual Campaign: An annual request for donations from a nonprofit's contact pool, usually conducted by mail, phone, or email. Gifts are usually "unrestricted" and fund basic operations at the nonprofit.

Appeal: An appeal usually refers to a single request for donations from a group of donors. A nonprofit that sends a letter trying to raise money for a new boat has just sent an "appeal." A follow-up phone-a-thon would be a separate appeal. Sending a new letter would be yet another appeal. Fundraisers like to keep track of specific appeals because it helps them track effectiveness. In the above scenario, each appeal could be tested for efficiency and response rate.

Ask: Usually refers to a direct solicitation for money. Often used as a noun, such as, "I have five asks scheduled today."

Call to Action: The actual request for an action on the part of the donor. Is it a call to volunteer? A call to go to the website? A call to write a check? Calls to action should be specific.

Campaign: A series of appeals for a specific goal, united by a common message and theme.

Development: Refers to fundraising, but also stewardship and cultivation of donors. "Advancement" can be considered synonymous.

Development Plan: A (usually) written plan of action for future fundraising activities, usually with a calendar and estimated budget numbers.

Donor Cultivation: The process of turning "the public" into donors and encouraging current donors to give larger gifts. It is usually done over time by both presenting the case for giving to the nonprofit and assessing the goals of the donor and looking for a match.

Donor Database: A database of donors and non-donors alike that tracks not only individuals, but their gifts and pledges.

Donor Pipeline: The process (often repeating) of cultivating a donor from identification to cultivation to "the ask" to stewardship.

Donor Pyramid: A visualization tool that describes the structure of donors to most nonprofits: a small handful of large donors at the top, built on a base of many donors who give smaller gifts.

Gift: A donation of money, stock, or goods or services given in-kind.

In-Kind: A gift of goods (a new printer) or services (free accounting consulting). Usually does not apply to people volunteering outside of their professional expertise (an accountant who helps rake leaves is not giving an in-kind gift).

Recurring Gift: A gift set up by the donor to be given over time, usually in monthly, quarterly, or annual installments.

Restricted Gift: A gift that can be used only for a specific purpose, as established by the donor. "To set up a scholarship for underprivileged kids." "To fix the scoreboard." "To go toward professional development." Violation of the terms of the gift is a serious breach of trust with the donor and can cause possible legal action.

Pledge: An agreement that a donor will give a certain amount at a later date.

Self-Identify: The process by which people indicate they are interested in your nonprofit's mission. This could mean giving on your website (unasked), asking to join your mailing list, or attending an event.

Stewardship: The process of thanking a donor, both in private and in public for a gift to your nonprofit.

Touch: A communication in virtually any form from your nonprofit to a donor or potential donor. If tracked, touches can tell you whether a donor will be receptive to an ask. Generally speaking, the more quality touches, the more a donor will be receptive.

Unrestricted Gift: A gift given with no guidelines from the donor. It is still restricted, however, in the sense that your nonprofit, as a charitable organization, is obligated to spend it toward your mission. The key is that the *donor* has not restricted it.

ABOUT THE AUTHOR

When he was just 23, Erik Hanberg was hired to run a non-profit arts organization with an annual budget just over $600,000. Two years later, he had increased the budget to $800,000, and increasing fundraising more than 400%.

Since then he has worked in development at a multi-million dollar non-profit and has volunteered on many boards.

He is currently the Executive Director of a small civic non-profit and sits on the distribution committee for a foundation that gives away more than $200,000 a year. In 2011, he was elected to a six year term on the Metro Parks Tacoma Board of Commissioners.

9 781475 205213